The Transformation of a Trillion Dollar Industry

How Demographics, Technology, and Unbridled Immigration will Change the U.S. Economy Forever Beginning in 2030

RODNEY W. SCHULTZ

NEWMAN SPRINGS PUBLISHING
320 Broad Street
Red Bank, NJ 07701

First originally published by Newman Springs Publishing 2019

ISBN 978-1-64531-263-5 (Paperback)
ISBN 978-1-64531-264-2 (Digital)

Printed in the United States of America

To my parents, Roger Sr. and Rosa Anna Schultz, who have been my mentors in life, business, and family. I will always owe you an invaluable debt of gratitude.

CONTENTS

FOREWORD

Thinking about the future is risky—but important. The future is inherently unknowable, but there are ways to reduce the knowledge gap. One way is to study history and to try to discover long term trends. History may not repeat, but it does rhyme. The better approach is to be a student of future prognostication and of demographics. There are a lot of smart people who spend their entire day researching and developing "educated guesses" about where the world is going. You should pay attention to them. Demographics is destiny. The number, location, ages, life expectancies, ethnicities, income, etc. of people on the planet is a very slow-moving data set. Over centuries, it may change suddenly due to external forces. Over decades, these numbers are forecast with great precision. Studying demographics yields clarity to the future of many aspects of society and business. In this book, Rodney Schultz has captured the essence of why forecasting the future direction of society is critical to the success or failure of a business, especially a construction business.

Thirty years ago I gave a speech to a large assemblage of contractors entitled, "Mega Trends in Construction." Variations of that speech are still given today around the country. Rodney has written a book that includes an in-depth approach to a more modern way of looking at running a successful construction business. He focuses on the future and why researching and anticipating societal changes are critical to survival in the next few decades. Also included in this book are insights and advice on how key changes will revolutionize the way construction businesses function. The biggest of these is technological transformation. After 40 years of stagnation, technology is finally being applied to the design and construction process. Billions of dollars are being invested in trying to improve the efficiency and productivity of this industry. About 1970, Alvin Toffler wrote a book, "Future Shock", which predicted that future would be driven not just by change, but by the speed of change. The speed of change in construction has been glacial, but it is poised to accelerate.

Also, the attitudes, values, goals, and expectations of the younger generations are changing how firms are organized, managed and how the leaders' function. Attracting, training, and retaining a workforce today and into the future is going to require dramatically different strategic and leadership skills than in the past. It will require a completely different way of thinking, engaging with employees and customers, and it will require completely different business models.

In "The Transformation of a Trillion Dollar Industry," Rodney has issued a call to arms and provided a roadmap to a new model of success in an industry that has changed very little since the Middle Ages. A combination of technology, demographics, societal attitudes, and new business models will drive dramatic change over the next few decades. The construction industry firms that respond to the new world order will thrive, those who do not will cease to exist.

Hugh L Rice
Senior Chairman
FMI Corporation

PROLOGUE

Have you ever wondered to yourself as an individual, student, business owner, executive, or entrepreneur what the world is going to be like for your remaining days here on earth? I do all the time.

What if I told you, with research and the help of other futurists, I could predict the future with a certain degree of accuracy; would you believe me? Maybe! But like most reasonable and rationale people, you would be a bit skeptical for sure, which is what I would encourage you to be.

Knowing what lies ahead in the future, regardless of how reasonable or remote the predictions may seem to appear, provides individuals, students, businesses owners, executives, and entrepreneurs a distinct competitive advantage for anyone wanting to spend the necessary time to do their own research for what might actually occur, especially, if a particular prediction that interests you is not too far out into the future. In fact, the closer a prediction of interest is to present day, the more curious most people become from a personal and financial perspective.

Take Steve Jobs's vision for the future for example. In 1977, his company, Apple, launched its first commercially viable product, the Apple II. Thirty-four years later, Mr. Jobs's decides to do the unthinkable and take on the powerful music and entertainment industries because in his mind he felt the world should be able to listen to music and watch movies whenever and where ever they wanted and in cost effect manner. As a result, in 2001, Apple introduces iTunes. Eight months later, Apple introduces the iPod—and the rest as they say is history.

Now can you just imagine how many people along the way shook their heads in disbelief at Mr. Jobs's visions and, in turn, failed to be proactive by doing their own research to see if his ideas were in fact viable or not?

Two things you have to understand about this book. First and foremost, most of what is being discussed here in terms of what lies ahead for the US economy, in particular the construction industry, is not new, some is, but the vast majority has been accumulated through exhaustive research and the public domain. In fact, I can say for certain that most everything you read in this book has been said or written about at least once by futurists and/or experts and is more real than it is prognostication.

The second thing about this book is that it takes the reader on a fascinating journey through the eye of a $1.2 trillion industry, i.e., construction, that I've been associated with my entire adult life, embracing lessons learned from the past, impacts being felt today, and future disruptions that are certainly coming in the not so distant tomorrow. It's also a journey that most futurist and forward thinkers will tell you is not going to be a pleasant one for a number of reasons, and one that most everyone living today in the US will be taking in one form or another as they go about their day whether they like it or not.

Viewed as a microcosm of the entire US economy, the construction industry is not immune from the myriad of social, cultural, political, and technological changes being forecasted on the horizon as demographic shifts impact how individuals will live and work. It is also one of very few sectors of the US economy that is most representative of the country's social diversity and interdependencies on various cultures manifested over the past century.

Like most of the US economy starting around the year 2030, construction is an industry that will start to see dramatic shifts in how it goes about meeting the future demand of its customers. Shifts that will require a massive overhaul on how the industry simultaneously tries to manage, market, and deliver its goods and services. For example:

- Starting in 2030, as the US population ages, international immigration is projected to overtake the "natural increase" (the excess of natural births over deaths) as the primary driver of population growth.

- Starting 2030, as the US population ages, the number of deaths are projected to rise substantially, which will slow the country's natural growth rate for decades to come.
- Starting in 2030, net international migration, i.e., immigration, is projected to overtake the country's "natural increase" even as levels of immigration are projected to remain relatively flat for the foreseeable future.

Starting in the decade of the 2030s, actual demographic milestones in the US population will mark the most transformative period in US history, thanks in large part to (a) Baby Boomers aging into their twilight years, (b) advancements in technology, and (c) an ever-increasing illegal immigrant population requiring, and in some areas demanding, that social services (including voting rights) be provided to them even though they have never provided any contribution to the public coffers for years. It will also be a decade that will eventually solidify, forever, a fractured two-party political system that will not be able to withstand the test of time.

Beyond the decade of the 2030s, the US population is projected to grow at a much slower pace, age considerably, and eventually become more racially and ethnically diverse. By the year 2035, despite a slowing population growth, the US population will see older adults actually outnumber children for the first time ever, while the global international population will continue to grow at a very stagnant pace.

As reasonably predictable as all this may sound, there are also a number of other predictions that should be taken into consideration as the decade of the 2030s quickly approaches and the demographics of the US continues to shift and evolve:

- Although the US economy has been shifting away from being a manufacturing-based economy to a service-based economy since the 1980s, hi-tech manufacturing, along with a spattering of conventional manufacturing, is expected to take hold throughout the US due to rising labor costs and subsequent labor shortages in Asia and Europe, and better trade deals being renegotiated by the current administration.

- The US will continue to lead the world in IT innovation, along with digital-based integration and application systems as advancements in emerging economies like "Sharing," "Streaming," "Gig," "Cloud," "Big Data," and "Artificial Intelligence" begin to take hold.

- With its access to vast amount of natural resources, the US will continue to be a leader in energy production.

- The US will continue to lead the world in science, biomedical, and pharmaceutical research where the advancement of new drugs, medical procedures and equipment will extend life expectancies worldwide.

- Supported by a politically motivated mainstream media that embraces the exploitation of sensationalism and conflict versus simply investigating and reporting the facts, the current two-party political system, which dominates all levels of government, will continue to decay into an entrenched tribalism, ultimately rendering all U.S. governing bodies untenable for decades to come as half the country's population sides with a more socialist agenda while the other half remains steadfastly moderate to conservative.

- The US will continue to the beacon for liberty and independence for all emerging democracies around the world. However, economically, with the need to raise taxes at all levels of the US government, e.g., federal, state, county, and city, in order to support a socially acceptable and/or modified economic system, the US will begin to struggle monetarily in the coming decades as the US debt, unsustainable entitlement programs, and outdated immigration policies, continue to be ignored by an established two-party political system focused more on self-preservation and power than the needs of the country at large.

- Business failures in the US will rise over the next two decades as older generations with limited saving for retirement years struggle to start and operate their own businesses with limited funds to cover operational and living expenses.

- The South and West regions of the US will continue to see unprecedented growth while the Midwest and Northeast regions will continue to experience slow growth or no growth at all.

- States like Florida, Georgia, Texas, and North Carolina, with pro-growth tax policies for individuals and corporations, will benefit from a high rate of population growth, while a large number of states in the Midwest and Northeast that are currently plagued by higher taxes and a crumbling infrastructure will continue to see sharp declines in their population.

- Driven by a more progressive attitude from customers looking for value, immigrants willing to work for lower wages, and an existing workforce migrating to the South and West, unionize labor, i.e., collective bargaining, will over time be replaced by a more cooperative and competitive form of labor/management relations where wages and benefits are closely tied to qualifications and actual levels of productivity.

- China's economy will begin to dramatically slow within the next thirty years due to its exceedingly low fertility rates, creating wide labor shortages and higher labor cost, and as a result, returning hi-tech manufacturing to the US economy and pushing lower-wage manufacturing to emerging continents like Africa and parts of Central and South America.

- As European demographics continue to shift and be transformed by relatively open immigration policies, many countries will struggle economically as the effects of labor shortages, higher labor costs, and lower productivity start to unfold.

- As the world's global economy slowly transforms itself with advancements of the digital age, currency, as a medium for economic exchange, will give way to new and more secure ways for commerce to take place.
- Sociotechnical systems (STS) will become the new revolution in how organizational structures become more operational alignment, synergistic, interdependent, and integrated from a digital perspective. All unnecessary movements of the hands and feet, along with unnecessary thought processing, will be replaced by robotics, automation, artificial intelligence, aerial drones, and IT.
- As future generations of digital platforms come online in conjunction with three transformative technologies: "cloud," "social," and "mobile", commerce around the world will become increasingly interdependent and seamlessly transactional. As a result, costs incurred for business travel will become unnecessary and virtually eliminated in the coming decades.
- A large majority of "cost of living" and/or minimum wage service-based jobs will gradually be eliminated and replaced by robotics, advancements in automation, and artificial intelligence. As these types of jobs become harder to find, a large percentage of the unskilled population will turn to criminal activities as a means to survive.
- Paper-based business operations will eventually cease to exist by the end of the decade of the 2030s, replaced by digital technology, systems, and expanded storage capacity.
- Although socially preferred by most developed countries, sources of alternative and/or renewable energy will continue to be promoted regardless of their commercial viability.
- As the speed of digital processing increases the use of algorithms will play a more dominant role in consumer marketing, completing complex calculation, data processing, and automated reasoning.
- "Bricks and mortar" marketing of goods and services will be replaced by social media and driven by viral marketing

as future generations move to fully embrace and normalize digital communications, social interactions, and online commerce.

- Although an acceptable way for current generations to communicate and businesses to market their goods and services, mass social media outlets will become less reliable in terms of content, politically biased, and regulated over time as digital platforms become exploited by the mainstream media, individuals, activists, and organizational groups who have an axe to grind for one reason or another.

- Fragmented relationships between manufacturing, design, installation, and supply chain management will become fully integrated, both vertically and horizontally, adding value to customers while accelerating deliverables at much lower costs.

- From healthcare to industrial materials and applications, 3D printing, copying, and manufacturing will become the next frontier for molecular imaging innovation.

- The language barriers in the US, along with other developed countries, will continue to get worse, not better, creating an ever-widening communication gap between individuals, consumers, owners, managers, and supervisors, as the lack of effective immigration policies plague countries and polarize political parties.

- For the foreseeable future, a disproportionately large portion of lower waged, manual, and blue-collar jobs will be consumed by the international immigrant (particularly Hispanic) and Black populations of the US economy, while the predominantly higher educated natural-born US citizens and Asian population, along with a disproportionately low number of Hispanics and Blacks, will consume marginally higher-paying jobs.

- Automobile sales in the US, particularly combustion engines, will be under extreme pressure due to late Generation X and Generation Y's propensity to find and use alternative sources of transportation.

- Although it would be reasonable to assume that the U.S. housing market over the next fifty years and beyond should be relatively strong given the projected size of Generations X, Y, and Z's impact on the economy, enhanced by the fact that life expectancy in the U.S. is expected to increase with advancements in medicine and healthcare, the reality is the housing market will remain unstable at best. Saddled with ever-increasing amounts of student loan and credit card debt, potential home buyers in the U.S. will not be able to afford the financial costs associated with owing their own homes while at the same time meeting their previous obligations, and, trying to maintain an acceptable standard of living.
- The amount of death services to be provided in the US will nearly double until the turn of the next century.
- Marijuana will be one of the largest cash crops on the international market due to its legalization and perceived medical benefits.
- Because of lax immigration policies—i.e., laws—and the need to have some means to supporting themselves, unemployed immigrants from Mexico and Central America will expand and strengthen existing gang activity over the coming decades, making the US a relatively unsafe place to live in a number of major metropolitan areas.

So why is all this important to know, especially for students, business owners, entrepreneurs, and executives?

It's important to know because the US economy doesn't appear to be ready for the demographic shifts about to occur starting twelve short years from now. For decades, many sectors of the US economy, like construction, have shown that even when demographic shifts to the supply and demand of goods and services do get recognized (case in point, a declining workforce in construction that has been occurring since the 1980s) nothing truly tangible, or effective, seems to get done in a timely manner in order to solve global concerns.

It's not that well-intentioned politicians or industry leaders don't try to make positive changes, because many do, but it's because the US economy, like construction, has become so large and fragmented that it's difficult to find a single or aligned voice for any global initiative to be enacted and/or viewed as a benefit to all participants.

Time for a Mental Note

Since the late 1980s, a large portion of the work put in place in the US, particularly in the Midwest and Northeast, was installed by a unionized workforce. This was also true for the manufacturing base of the US economy. But as the US population started migrating to the South and West in the late 1980s and early 1990s, the workforce in these areas expanding areas became less unionized. Moreover, as the economies of the South and West continued to grow and prosper, so too did merit shop (non-union) contracting, where today, unionized labor in construction is less than 20 percent of the overall workforce.

As the late 1990s, early 2000s, started to unfold, previous generations of organized, i.e., union, construction workers began to migrate to South and West as well to find work and prepare for their retirement in the coming years. It was also a time when newer generations of eligible and prospective tradespeople started to shy away from a career in the construction industry in pursuit of other more appealing occupations that didn't require a manual labor component to it. As a result, the construction industry now faces a serious labor shortage of available, and qualified, trade supervisors and workers which is starting to severely impact the overall industry.

But being slow to react to demographic changes is not the half of it. When industries, like construction, are so slow to respond to the future demands of its customers, many new, existing, and small business owners feel unprotected from the economic environment that they all of a sudden find themselves in; and in turn, give up any hope of ever being competitive again. Remember the mom and pop lumber yards and hardware stores that supplied the construction industry and "Do it Yourselfers" until big box stores like Home Depot and Lowes started spring up as if overnight. It's simply a fact, that when the barriers to entry into a market are low, failure rates tend to be exceedingly high for business owners who are unaware, unsuspecting, underfunded, or unable to compete. Just look at what's happening to the centuries old taxicab and livery driver businesses with companies like Uber and Lyft now competing for passengers.

Time for a Mental Note

On May 27, 2018, two reporters, Nikita Stewart and Luis Ferre'-Sadurni, wrote a story for The New York Times entitled, "Another Taxi Driver in Debt Takes His Life. That's 5 in 5 Months."

Here's that story:

On a corner of 86th Street and East End Avenue in Manhattan on Sunday, three posters for a missing man were still hanging on a lamp post about a block from the East River.

That was where the police found the man's parked taxicab, the biggest investment of his life. The man, Yu Mein Chow, had taken out a loan seven years ago to buy a $700,000 medallion that gave him the right to operate a cab.

Mr. Chow, 56, who lived in Queens and went by the nickname "Kenny," disappeared on May 11. His body was found floating in the East River about nine miles south, near the Brooklyn Bridge, on Wednesday. Friends and family members believe Mr. Chow jumped to his death, adding to a string of apparent suicides of traditional taxi and livery drivers in the city. It marked *the fifth suicide in* just over five months. *The medical examiner has not yet determined a cause of death.*

New York City's cab industry, dependent on the market value of the once-coveted taxi medallion, has been upended by the proliferation of Uber *and other ride-sharing services. Drivers have been demanding changes at City Hall to protect their livelihood, but at least five cabbies have buckled under the strain of debt since December as others describe working 12- and 14-hour shifts to make up for the lost income. One driver* shot himself in February outside City Hall *after leaving* a message on Facebook *blaming the industry's demise on politicians.*

On Sunday, Richard Chow, Mr. Chow's older brother, went to the street where the police found the taxi as part of a vigil that drew dozens of the driver's friends and fellow cabbies on a bleak afternoon. He climbed the stone steps of nearby Carl Schurz Park and headed toward the iron fence on an esplanade that overlooks the river. "I loved my brother. He was very hard working. He loved his family," Mr. Chow managed to say before his voice broke and his eyes teared up. "That's all I want to say."

The medallion system was created to limit the number of cabdrivers, but ride-sharing apps have rendered it useless, said Bhairavi Desai, executive director of the New York City Taxi Workers Alliance. *Last year, data showed that more people used Uber than yellow cabs in the city. Once sold for more than $1 million, taxi medallions are now selling for as little as $175,000, according to* data collected by the Taxi and Limousine Commission.

Ms. Desai said she has been transformed into a part-time counselor to despondent drivers who call her in the wee hours of the morning and a part-time eulogist who talks to family and friends to share the stories of the deceased.

Born in Burma, Yu Mein Chow did not immediately take up taxi driving as a profession when he first moved to the United States as a young man. He became a jeweler, Ms. Desai said.

When the business he worked for closed, she said, "He had to reinvent himself. That's when he started to drive a taxi cab."

Mr. Chow bought a medallion in 2011, just as Uber was beginning to operate in New York City. By last year, Mr. Chow was realizing that his $700,000 investment was not paying off. He could not afford his daughter's college education. He could not afford the medical bills after his wife was diagnosed with cancer, Ms. Desai said.

Ms. Desai said Mr. Chow went to make a payment on his medallion loan a few days before he went missing. His credit card was declined.

On Sunday, mourners bowed their heads three times to honor their friend. Richard Chow grabbed a red flower and a white flower and walked toward the iron fence that divides the city from the choppy waters of the East River. More people followed, and together they threw flowers into the river.

Behind them, new posters they had hung on a pole read: "Rest in Peace. Beloved father, husband, brother, friend, NYC taxi driver."

In a September 2013 article published in *Forbes*, they listed the top five reasons why entrepreneurs fail:

1. Entrepreneurs are not really in touch with customers through deep dialogue.
2. Entrepreneurs are not able to create a real differentiation in the market, i.e., lack of unique value propositions.

3.   Entrepreneurs fail to communicate value propositions in clear, concise and compelling fashion.
4.   Leadership breakdown at the top, i.e., founder dysfunction.
5.   Entrepreneurs are unable to produce a profitable business model with revenue streams.

To me, the list in the *Forbes* article is reasonable, and definitely has some validity when viewed in the context of how businesses operate in today's economic and social environment. Take the construction industry for example, with its extremely low barriers to entry for entrepreneurs wanting to become contractors, where for decades, the $1.2 trillion industry has seen its fair share of contractors come and go at an alarming rate.

Regardless of size, location, or diversified service offering, three out of four (75 percent) construction contractors in the US fail within the first eighteen months of operation. A statistic, by the way, that is actually lower than the rate of business failures reported by *Bloomberg* in the past, where *Bloomberg* put the rate at eight out of ten (80 percent) for entrepreneurs who startup a small business fail within the first eighteen months. And if those failure rates are not concerning enough, over the next fifty years, beginning in 2030, the frequency of business failures in the US is expected to get even worse as the number of aging entrepreneurs with limited savings compound the failure rate by starting up their own small businesses during their expected retirement years. Small business that will most likely be underfunded and focused on providing products and services geared more toward older generations than the more recent ones. Why? Because generational entrepreneurs are more likely to focus on what they know and what they're used to, which in turn, dictates who their target consumer will be.

Arguably, the next three decades will find the US economy in a constant state of flux and disruption for roughly one-third of the population who were born prior to the tech revolution. Meaning, two-thirds of the US population will not only be tech-savvy, but they will also be increasingly more accepting to social diversity and language barriers created by an never ending flow of immigrants.

While one-third of the population will become increasingly frustrated by the overwhelming economic, social, and cultural changes being taken out of their control, two-thirds of the population will be embracing a new value system that will include social and cultural diversity, as well English no longer being considered the primary language everyone speaks throughout the country. As a result of this generational divergence, older generations will eventually find contentment within their own communities by holding onto a value system they have come to know and be comfortable with, while newer generations struggle within themselves to find the right path that is socially and culturally tolerant and acceptable to all.

Time for a Mental Note

Two friends speaking Spanish were told to speak English. A bystander stepped in to help

(CNN) — *A woman is being hailed a hero after confronting another woman who was criticizing two friends for speaking Spanish to each other at a store in Colorado.*

Fabiola Velasquez, 30, told CNN that she and her friend Isabel Nava Marin were at a City Market supermarket in Rifle on Monday afternoon. The two women were in an aisle chatting with each other in Spanish when another woman "aggressively" approached them.

According to Velasquez, the woman, identified by police as Linda Dwire, 64, told the two friends that if they lived in the United States, they "had to speak in English."

That's when 30-year-old Kamira Trent intervened.

Velasquez took video of part of the exchange between Dwire and Trent and shared it on Facebook.

As of Thursday night, the video had been seen about a million times. Around 2,900 Facebook users have commented and overwhelmingly praised Trent for stepping in to defend the two friends.

"Don't harass people," Trent said in the video as Dwire got closer, pointing a finger at her. At one point, Dwire got close enough that she touched Trent, who pushed Dwire's arm and started to back away, saying, "Do not—I'm calling the cops."

Dwire then told Trent, "You know what, you come from a different generation." Trent cuts Dwire off and replied, "No I do not, I have respect."

The two women kept walking down the aisle. Dwire can be heard saying "you will lose this country," while Trent said "this woman needs to be escorted out of here," later adding, "you do not harass Hispanic women."

Dwire was arrested and charged with two counts of bias-motivated harassment, according to the Rifle Police Department.

In the police affidavit, Sgt. Carlos Cornejo wrote that when he arrived at the scene and talked to Dwire, the woman stated "she found it offensive" that Velasquez and her friend were speaking Spanish.

Dwire also stated that she approached the two friends and asked if they lived in the United States and if they liked it, adding she also told them to speak English and be American.

According to the affidavit, Cornejo also stated that Dwire "went on to say that she was offended because when you speak another language you divide yourself. She stated that it gives her the idea that they want to bring their country here and want her to conform to their country."

Cornejo added Dwire said she was exercising her right to freedom of speech.

In the affidavit, Cornejo said he saw the video Velasquez took. The document has a screen shot of the video that shows Dwire pointing her finger at Trent and Trent pushing Dwire away.

Dwire was transported and booked to Garfield County Jail. She was later released. CNN reached out to Dwire for comment by phone on Thursday and left a message, and did not get a call back.

CNN also reached out to Trent on Thursday by phone and via social media but she has not responded.

In a Facebook post published on Monday, Velasquez wrote, in Spanish, about her experience: "I always saw the videos on social media and they made me angry, and today when it happened to me I can say that I felt a lot of helplessness."

Velasquez told CNN she would not like something similar to happen to others, but added that if it does happen "they have rights and they can call the police."

"Many times [the] Hispanic community does not feel secure asking for help."

CNN also reached out to City Market on Thursday by phone and left messages, which were not returned.

What this all means for most sectors of the US economy, in particular sectors like construction, is that unless current and future generations of business owners can find a way to bridge the generational, cultural, and societal gaps being created by the significant challenges ahead, there is zero chance that the future demands of customers will ever be met to their satisfaction and within a reasonable timeframe. Demands by customers that will be predicated on: (a) cultural dynamics; (b) digital compliance; (c) size of deliverable;

(d) effective communications between multiple languages; (e) speed, accuracy; (f) integration; (g) innovation; (h) convenience; (i) social interactions; and (j) value-add propositions.

Unfortunately, though, and for reasons I'll explain throughout this book, most traditional business owners, including contractors in the construction industry, see absolutely no need to (a) prepare for the language barriers currently being created between a workforce of English and Spanish speaking employees, (b) embrace automation technology that will enhance their deliverables and aid in the labor shortages effecting their particular industry, (c) innovate new and useful products and/or services, (d) becoming a value-added service provider, or (e) find productive ways to close the generational gaps being created between old school and new school employees as individuals continue to live and work longer.

If I'm scaring you—i.e., Baby Boomer owners, managers, supervisors, and employees, about what lies ahead for the decades to come—good! I need to be!

Am I worried about what the future has in store for the US economy as a whole, in particular the trials and tribulations that lie ahead for my industry, construction? Very much so!

Do I believe both the US economy, and in particular construction industry, has the necessary resiliency to adapt and overcome any troubled times ahead? Absolutely I do!

Generational Demographics

Looking back over the past one hundred years of the US economy, with a particular interest paid to industries like construction, there has been arguably nineteen economic recessions, the last being the Great Recession of 2007 through 2009, with each occurring within three to five years of one another on average and lasting anywhere from one to four years at a time.

During this same period of time, the US found itself engaged in six major military conflicts that span seven of the nineteen periods of economic recession. But unlike a recession, where the demand for goods and services fall off sharply, military conflicts create a different kind of impact to industries like construction where the supply of manpower, material, and machinery becomes severely restricted as resources get redirected to supporting the war effort.

Thankfully, though, there has not been a major military conflict fought on US soil since before the turn of the twentieth century. However, this fact alone in no way diminished the impact soldiers had on the US economy as they returned home from abroad to start their lives all over again.

Starting with the GI Generation (1905 through 1924), the US population increased after the turn of the twentieth century by approximately 56.6 million people (of which, about 2.3 million are still alive today). Then the Silent Generation (1925 to 1944) came along with its 52.6 million births. Then the unthinkable happened over the next twenty years, 78 million were added compliments of the post-WWII Baby Boomer Generation (1945 through 1964). And to this very day, the impacts of the Baby Boomer Generation are unprecedented and will continue to be for decades to come.

But hold on to your seats! If you think those three generations had a major impact on the US economy in recent decades, you haven't seen anything yet as the decade of the 2030s quickly approaches and Generations X and Y have their say on how the US economy will be impacted via goods and services demanded by consumers.

Coupled with the collective impacts of the aging three previous generations that came before them, along with Generation Z that is expected to be as large as the Baby Boomer Generation by the time 2024 ends, Generations X and Y will be churning through the US economy with an insatiable appetite, consuming products and services at a rate that's currently incalculable. Why? Because Generation X (1965 through 1984) added almost 82 million people (69 million natural born and 13 million from international immigration) to the already sizable US population. Generation Y (1985 through 2004) comes along and adds another 86 million people (79 million natural born and 7 million from international immigration) to the population. At no time in the country's history has there ever been an increase of this magnitude in population spanning two generations, which included 20 million foreign born citizens.

Here's a rule to always remember when trying to forecast shifts in any economy that Kenneth W. Gronbach mentions in his wonderful book entitled *Upside*: demographics (i.e., people), always precipitates economics (i.e., money and things).

Let's face it, people, i.e., customers, drive the world, not systems, not governments, and definitely not management styles. And as the older generations in our society will tell you, humans still have to verbally communicate with one another in order to survive, be productive, and remain safe. Not to mention the fact that humans have to be the ones to innovate, program artificial intelligence, and, maintain the robots of the future. Right? Not so fast!

Time for a Mental Note

Generations are predictable markets that consume typical goods and services as they age: Babies consume formula and diapers; children under ten consume clothing, candy, and cereal; teenagers consume fashion, soft drinks, and now video games; young adults in their twenties consume entertainment, cosmetics, and fashion; adults in their thirties consume houses, household goods and services, insurance, and automobiles; folks in their forties also consume houses (usually more expensive ones), household goods and services, boats, legal services, automobiles; those in their fifties consume second homes, more household goods and services, and travel; those in their sixties take cruises, and consume pharmaceuticals, and start planning for retirement; those in the seventies consume more pharmaceuticals and start downsizing to smaller more manageable homes; and those in their eighties and nineties look to move into assisted living facilities and consume funeral and death services.

Knowing what people consume at particular times in their life should make it relatively easy to predict with a reasonable degree of confidence, at any particular time in the future, what the demand for certain consumer products and services will be at their peaks. With that said, businesses today, and in the future, should really only have to ask themselves two questions when it comes to the potential demand by customers of their products or services:

1. How many people—i.e., potential customers—are there in my market?
2. Is that number getting bigger or smaller?

Common sense tells you that if you don't know how many people you're dealing with at a particular point in time, you simply have no idea what's driving the world, or market, from a demand perspective. But on the other hand, if you are keenly aware of the dynamics surrounding any given population, you will most be able to capitalize on what ultimately drives sales and opportunities. Here again, it's all about supply and demand.

Being able to understand shifting demographics not only prepares visionaries, entrepreneurs, business owners, and marketers for what's expected over the next horizon in terms of the demand for certain products and services, it is also the purest precursor for anyone to have looking for a successful future in business. Granted, it is one thing to meet an existing demand of customers, but it is a far different matter to anticipate what the demand will be at some point in the future. Visionaries, like a Steve Jobs, Henry Ford, Thomas Edison, and many other others, along with entrepreneurs, business owners, inventors, and marketers who are able to anticipate the future are the same ones who truly set themselves apart from any competition that may come along with a similar idea.

So what does all this have to do with the decade of the 2030s and beyond as it relates to the US economy, and in particular, industries like construction?

Starting in the decade of the 2030s, all generations prior to Generation X will most likely be retired and preparing to live out the remainder of their lives as comfortably as possible. They will do so unlike any group of retirees have done in the past because technology and the significant advancements in medicine will allow them to live longer and feel healthier in ways previous generation could have never imagined. From artificial hips, knees, elbows to safe and effective cataract surgery, living in pain as one gets older is something retirees will no longer have to worry about.

For business owners, executives, and entrepreneurs to dismiss what's predicted to happen in the US starting in the year 2030 is nothing short of being foolhardy. Granted not all futurists, research firms, and experts in various fields agree on everything, or at least the timeframe in which events are expected to occur, but they do agree on a number of things that individuals, business owners, executives, and entrepreneurs should all take stock in and start doing their own research.

For example, take some time and check out this list of prognostications and predictions from Google's top rated futurist, Mr.

Thomas Frey. Although, a number of Mr. Frey's prognostications and predictions may seem to be out there a bit, I'm relatively certain he's done his homework as you should do for yourself.

- By 2030, over 80 percent of all doctor visits will have been replaced by automated exams.
- By 2030, over 90 percent of all restaurants will use some form of a 3D food printer in their meal preparations.
- By 2030, over 10 percent of all global financial transactions will be conducted through Bitcoin or Bitcoin-like crypto currencies.
- By 2030, we will see a growing number of highways designated as driverless-vehicle only.
- By 2030, a Chinese company will become the first to enter the space tourism industry by establishing regular flights to their space hotel.
- By 2030, the world's largest Internet company will be in the education business, and it will be a company we have not heard of yet.
- By 2030, over 20 percent of all new construction will be "printed" buildings.
- By 2030, over 2 billion jobs will have disappeared, freeing up talent for many new fledgling industries.
- By 2030, a new protest group will have emerged that holds anti-cloning rallies, demonstrating against the creation of "soul-less humans."
- By 2030, we will see the first city to harvest 100 percent of its water supply from the atmosphere.
- By 2030, world religions will make a resurgence, with communities of faith growing by nearly 50 percent over what they are today.
- By 2030, over 50 percent of all traditional colleges will collapse, paving the way for an entire new education industry to emerge.

- By 2030, we will see a surge of Micro Colleges spring to life, each requiring less than six months of training and apprenticeship to switch professions.
- By 2030, scientists will have perfected an active cross-species communication system, enabling some species to talk to each other as well as humans.
- By 2030, we will see the first hurricane stopped by human intervention.
- By 2030, we will see wireless power used to light up invisible lightbulbs in the middle of a room.
- By 2030, we will see the first demonstration of a technology to control gravity, reducing the pull of gravity on an object by as much as 50 percent.
- By 2030, democracy will be viewed as inferior form of government.
- By 2030, traditional police forces will be largely automated out of existence with less than 50 percent of current staffing levels on active duty.
- By 2030, over 90 percent of all libraries will offer premium services as part of their business model.
- By 2030, forest fires will have been reduced to less than 5 percent of the number today with the use of infrared drone monitoring systems.
- By 2030, over 30 percent of all cities in the US will operate their electric utilities as micro grids.
- By 2030, we will have seen a number of global elections with the intent of creating a new global mandate, forcing world leaders to take notice.
- By 2030, traditional pharmaceuticals will be replaced by hyper-individualized medicines that are manufactured at the time they are ordered.
- By 2030, we will have seen the revival of the first mated pair of an extinct species.
- By 2030, swarms of micro flying drones—swarmbots— will be demonstrated to assemble themselves as a type

of personal clothing, serving as a reconfigurable fashion statement.

- By 2030, marijuana will be legalized in all fifty states in the US and half of all foreign countries.
- By 2030, cable television will no longer exist.
- By 2030, a small number of companies will begin calculating their labor costs with something called "synaptical currency."
- By 2030, it will be common to use next generation search engines to search the physical world.
- By 2030, basic computer programming will be considered a core skill required in over 20 percent of all jobs.
- By 2030, we will have seen multiple attempts to send a probe to the center of the earth.
- By 2030, a form of tube transportation, inspired by Hyperloop and ET3, will be well on its way to becoming the world's largest infrastructure project.

I cannot stress enough how important it is for current and future business owners, executives, and entrepreneurs to understand the importance of staying on top of generational demographics, along with the demographic shifts that over time effect the supply and demand of all goods and services here in the US and around the world. And believe it or not, the odds of reasonably predicting the future are pretty high once you understand that groups of people share the needs and interests as they march through their individual life cycle. Recognizing those needs and interests, as well as with their respective magnitudes, is how business owners, executives, and entrepreneurs prepare themselves to meet the future demands of customers, while simultaneously staying ahead of the competition.

Techs Impact on the US Economy

As we have already witnessed over the past thirty years or so, technology has transformed how humans all over the world communicate and interact with one another. But what is most uncertain at this point in time, and as the decade of the 2030s quickly approaches, is just how technology is going to affect the daily lives of each individual in this country, as well as those around the world, as the US economy catapults its way forward into an unchartered landscape.

Changing at seemingly breakneck speed, the digital (a.k.a. information) age continues to race into the future leaving behind generations of uninformed and unappreciative owners, managers, supervisors, workers, and individuals used to the "bricks and mortar" way of living their lives and conducting business. Owners, managers, supervisors, workers, and individuals who are living and working longer, and with a number of whom who really don't share the same level of enthusiasm, or acumen, for the advancements in technology as more recent generations do. Believe it or not, some folks just like the way things are or used to be, so to say there's a generation gap being created is an understatement.

But like it or not, owners, managers, supervisors, workers, and individuals all live in the age of digital platforms, artificial intelligence, and algorithms these days aided in part by easy and convenient access to the internet. From news, sports and weather being reported and distributed, shopping for goods and services, research, investing, and communicating with others, everything is now done online and through digital platforms that are conveniently accessible to anyone with capable hardware.

Where once iconic "bricks and mortar" brand names like GE, K-Mart, Sears, Toys R US, Pan Am, Blockbuster, Oldsmobile, Borders, and Woolworth's were the darlings on Madison Avenue, tech-based companies like Facebook, Apple, Amazon, Netflix, and Google have now taken the international markets by storm. Tech-based companies that now affect everyone's daily life like no other social revolution has ever done before.

Thanks to the digital and electronic age, tech-based companies are springing up everywhere, from Silicon Valley to Wall Street, where the most valuable company in the world, Apple, recently topped the trillion market cap mark. To witness such a meteoric rise of a business sector revolution of the US economy is certainly something that doesn't come along very often.

Take for example, the last revolution to hit the worldwide stage in 1760, The Industrial Revolution. A revolution that arguably took one hundred years for it to reach its full potential with the invention machine tools and mass-production techniques. Now contrast The Industrial Revolution to the Tech revolution of the last thirty short years where tech-based innovations hadn't even become commercially viable yet. Today, technology changes every three to six years, if not sooner, with single roll-outs of new products and/or services across the globe. That's how fast technology is changing the world.

As much as business owners, entrepreneurs, and in some cases inventors, in the past liked to believe in the principle of "Build it and they will come," it truly wasn't a viable short-term business proposition if no one knew or understood the demographics of a target market. Back then, and not so far in the distant past, inventions, ideas, and concepts took time to become commercially viable, socially acceptable, and ultimately successful.

A great example of this is the electric toaster invented in 1893. The only problem with inventing a toaster 1893 was the fact there wasn't a commercially viable use for it. It wasn't until 1928, thirty-five years later, when sliced bread was introduced to the marketplace by the bakery industry. But today, technology, with its algorithms and viral marketing data, is changing all this, and for the better.

Time for a Mental Note

Until around the year 2000, it used to take between twenty-five and thirty years for a new invention or technology to reach the market and become commercially viable. Today, we are now seeing this timeframe cut by almost half, if not more. One day you go out and buy the latest and greatest laptop computer. Two years later you take it in for a repair or some form of upgrade and the tech behind the counter explains to you that they can't help because the unit is an older model. Happens all the time in the electronics world.

Take cell phones for example. Most of us who were around in the 1980s remember the first generation cell phone. A large, clunky, and expensive gadget that was unique, but not very convenient in terms of storage, mobility, or commercial viability at the time. Twenty short years later, cell phones and their usage charges became so affordable and convenient that most adults, along with the vast majority of teens, had one, and the cell phone quickly became the primary source for communications.

Now, today, in addition to using cell phones to sync up stored data to personal computers, consumers around the world communicate using smartphones, iPads, tablets, as well as a whole host of other electronic gadgets, mediums, and digital platforms. Even video games now provide IM (instant messaging) and chat room capabilities where multiple participants can interact with one another in languages that are new, abbreviated, encrypted, and becoming more and more socially acceptable, e.g., emojis.

What's important for businesses, especially contractors, to understand about digital platforms, is that they extend well beyond the technology sector of the US economy. They are now the new horizon for all things marketing and deliverable. Online retailers like,

Amazon, eBay, along with others, are without question transforming how businesses advertise, i.e., viral marketing, and distribute their products and services to consumers.

As technology continues to revolutionize the way individuals and businesses communicate and interact with one another, companies around the globe have recognized the need to create their own digital platform as a means to accelerate their own reach to new markets. Digital platform models comprised of providers, consumers, and employees that create a medium for exchange of goods, services, and social interaction. But here's the rub. If business owners, entrepreneurs, and individuals today are not preparing themselves to work within digital platform models in the future, they are absolutely going to struggle to meet the future demands of customers, and by all accounts, be left behind by competitors who do embrace the digital age.

What this means is that in order for a business, i.e., contractors, to prosper in the future as a particular industry moves into the next generation of viability, they will have to become keenly aware of the immense power found within emerging digital platforms. Digital platforms related to viral marketing, consumer recommendations, social awareness, and personal relationships to name just a few.

Take social media platforms as an example.

Although social media appears to have created an entire generation of narcissists, it is quickly becoming the most convenient and readily available mass media outlet for public service announcements, viral marketing, consumer reports, interpersonal communications, and online purchasing. Websites like, Twitter, Google, Facebook, Amazon, and Instagram (along with others) have all been setup in one form or another as digital platforms for businesses and/or individual consumers to interact with one another; and in a number of instances as a means for commercial exchange to take place in a convenient setting.

Time for Mental Note

There are three types of digital platforms:

a)   Social Platforms—which help facilitate social interactions and communication between individuals and businesses.
b)   Aggregation Platforms—which help facilitate transactions relating to data resources.
c)   Mobilization platforms—which help facilitate bringing individuals together in an attempt to develop long-term relationships and acquire shared goals and visions.

I cannot stress enough the power and influence digital platforms are having on the US economy, and are gearing up to have as the twenty-second century approaches. As business owners, entrepreneurs, students, and individuals, you have to be mindful of the fact that there is no turning back for most of these companies. Investments have already been made into these tech-based concepts and/or models to the point where financial markets today actually hinge on whether they succeed or not.

To be more precise, in recent years, innovation has introduced three transformative technologies: "cloud," "social," and "mobile." "Cloud" enables a global infrastructure for production that allows users to create content and applications. "Social" brings individuals together, while "mobile" devises allow connectivity to a global infrastructure. And as a result, entrepreneurs, employees/workers, and consumers become globally accessible through a mass medium in order to create a vehicle for content and commercial exchange aimed at a multitude of eventual buyers, sellers, and interactive participants.

But hold on a minute, what's going to happen to businesses needing to travel the globe to meet with customers and make sales calls? You guessed it. These three transformative technologies will all but eliminate the need for businesses to incur costs for travel in the coming decades.

Time for a Mental Note

Remember the 1989 United Airlines commercial where it starts out with an executive named Ben announcing to his sales group that an old friend of the company had just called and fired them after twenty years of doing business. The commercial then showed Ben passing out airline tickets to his various account managers who appeared to look surprised and perplexed at the whole dynamic of what was going on.

According to the longtime customer, he complained to Ben that instead of face-to-face communications between account managers and his employees continuing, where a handshake and personal contract embodied the company's personal touch, Ben's company had drifted away from the inconveniences of traveling in exchange for adopting the more convenient and impersonal approach of phone calls and faxes.

At the very end of the commercial one of salespeople asks Ben: "Ben, *where are you going?* Ben replied: *"To visit that old friend who fired us this morning."*

In today's world of business, and for generations to come, physical contact and/or interaction between employees and customers will be present to some extent, but it will not be as pervasive, and expected, as it has been for the past one hundred years or so. We are now in the digital age where the acceptance of emails, text messages, video conferencing, electronic signatures, and EDI are the acceptable forms in which employees and customers communicate, interact, and conduct most business activities.

Time for a Mental Note

"The best customer service is if the customer doesn't need to call, doesn't need to talk to you. It just works." (Jeff Bezos)

But beware, technology isn't stopping with making the conventional and mundane more convenient and productive. Within the next decade or so artificial intelligence (AI) will start to become the new norm in everyone's life. From UAVs (unmanned aerial vehicles, a.k.a. drones, flying overhead delivering packages and mail) to helping arrange dates between online daters, AI and AI-enabled features will begin to make life feel as though we're living with space aged Jetsons of the 1960s.

For business owners, executives, and entrepreneurs, especially in industries like construction, to assume science and technology won't be playing that big a role going forward in how they go about delivering the highest level of "value" and quality to customers, they really need to think again. The effects of social engineering is upon us and it's only going to get more invasive as technology expands its reach.

Time for a Mental Note

Social engineering is centralized planning used in an attempt to influence and/or manage social change to the point where the future behavior and development of a societal norms become regulated or conformed to a prescribed outcome. Social engineering can also become very troublesome to society as well, especially when unsuspecting and unwitting participants give up their personal and confidential information under deceptive and fraudulent pretenses.

To say that one day AI, algorithms, and social engineering will not be interlinked, influencing how individuals live and function is folly at best. AI alone, powered by advancements in technology and algorithms alike, where mechanical devices and machinery are programmed at the highest level of precision to emulate and/or reproduce the human decision making process, should be enough to give most everyone some pause to consider in terms of what might happen to individual liberties in the future. Add to this concern the potential of what creative and/or nefarious minded individuals could do with the vast reaches of social media if their goal was to somehow

alter the natural balance of predictable demographics and the anticipated behavior of society as a whole.

I know this all may sound counterintuitive to the value systems
steadfastly embraced by most business owners, executives, and entrepreneurs from generations prior to Generation X, but it is truly the
reality of the world we now live in. Technology is here to stay, and
whether or not individuals, business owners, executives, or entrepreneurs prior to Generation X want to accept the digital age and all
that comes with it in the coming years is up to them. However, time
is of the essence, and if individuals, business owners, executives, and
entrepreneurs prior to Generation X wait too long, the decision will
ultimately be made for them.

Unbridled Immigration: The Quiet Invasion Making Its Indelible Mark on the Future of the US Economy

As many politicians like to remind their constituents, and the constituents of the opposing party, when it comes to the immigration debate, "America is a land of immigrants," which technically, has not been an accurate statement for almost a century now as the rate of natural born citizens started to multiply by significant numbers just after the turn of the twentieth century. But that as it may, this country is about to come full circle starting in the decade of 2030 when the US population shifts back to becoming a land of immigrants.

Time for a Mental Note

The United States became home to a massive wave of immigrants during the colonial era, and then again during the latter part of the eighteenth century and early nineteenth century. Many immigrants came to America to escape religious prosecution, and, to seek greater economic prosperity. Between the seventeenth and nineteenth centuries, hundreds of thousands of African slaves were transported to America against their will. Then, in 1882, the Chinese Exclusion Act significantly restricted immigration.

The reason why the immigration debate is so important to understand by business owners, executives, entrepreneurs, and legal citizens of the US is because by the turn of the twenty-second century our country will have unwittingly transformed itself into a predominantly bilingual (English and Spanish) speaking culture and away from a predominantly English speaking one. And because of this unwitting transformation to a predominantly influential and bi-lingual Hispanic/Latin culture, chaos, conflict, confusion, and crime will all play a significant role for decades to come as US demographics shift to a more diversified environment.

Hard to believe? Let's look at the reality of the situation.

For the past thirty years or so, there has been a constant stream of growing and unaccounted for immigrants living in the US illegally, in additional to the 20 million or so who have entered the country legally since 1965. Add to these numbers on any given day, a wave of illegal immigrants from Mexico, Central and South America traversing their way toward the US Mexican border by whatever means necessary.

Time for a Mental Note

In an October 20, 2018, article written in *The New York Times* by Maya Averbuch and Kirk Semple, entitled, *"Migrant Caravan Continues North, Defying Mexico and U.S."* it is made clear how immigrants from Central America are bound and determined to defy all warnings from the US government not to come this country without going through the proper channels.

> *TAPACHULA, Mexico — In open defiance of the Mexican and American governments, thousands of Central American undocumented migrants, most of a* caravan *that has been heading toward the*

United States for more than a week, resumed their journey on Sunday in southern Mexico.

The Mexican government, which has been under pressure by President Trump to stop the caravan, *had ordered the migrants to submit to processing by the immigration authorities at a legal border crossing.*

But thousands chose instead to move on — part of a group of people who had been stopped at the Mexican border this week after having traveled for several days, most from their homes in Honduras.

Most of the migrants on the move on Sunday — by one local government estimate more than 7,000 people — had crossed the border illegally in recent days by swimming or rafting across the Suchiate River, *which separates Guatemala from Mexico.*

They gathered in the central square in the Mexican border city of Ciudad Hidalgo on Saturday and voted by a show of hands to continue their journey north despite their undocumented status.

"We want to get to the United States," said Maria Irias Rodriguez, 17, a migrant from Tegucigalpa, Honduras, who was traveling with her 8-month-old daughter, 2-year-old son and husband. "If they stop us now, we'll just come back a second time."

She said she had waited at the border until mid-Saturday but became desperate at how long it was taking to be processed.

On Sunday afternoon, Mr. Trump took to Twitter again to address the caravan, saying that those migrants seeking asylum must first apply in Mexico. "If they fail to do that, the U.S. will turn them away," he said, and then returned to the issue on Monday.

But Mexican officials have said migrants seeking asylum are under no legal obligation to apply in Mexico.

Under a proposed bilateral agreement *that the Trump administration has discussed with Mexican officials, United States border officials would be able to legally turn back asylum seekers who first pass through Mexico, forcing them to seek protection south of the border.*

In southern Mexico on Sunday, officials encouraged the migrants to apply for asylum or otherwise seek legal immigration status in Mexico, but they made barely any effort to halt the migrants as they walked along a main highway. Federal police officers were at times present on the road, monitoring the procession, and a police helicopter circled overhead, but the authorities allowed the procession to carry on unimpeded.

At one point a senior migration official standing in the back of a police pickup truck urged the migrants to register themselves with the authorities and seek legal immigration status, saying that the migrants could not cross the country without documentation.

But people said they feared being deported and the group kept moving north. By evening most of the migrants, extremely weary from the arduous walk, had reached the city of Tapachula, about a 20-mile journey by road from Ciudad Hidalgo.

The group planned to continue their journey north on Monday.

The caravan is part of a tradition of mass migrations, often organized by advocacy groups, meant to provide safety in numbers to migrants, who face many threats to their safety along the per-

ilous migrant trail. Many say they are fleeing economic distress and violence in their homelands.

Such caravans have usually numbered in the hundreds and have passed unnoticed. But the current caravan, by far the largest on record, has angered Mr. Trump, who has seized on it as a campaign issue *to fire up his base before the midterm elections.*

While other caravans have generally withered as they have progressed north, this one has grown, perhaps in part as a result of all the media attention it has received.

The Mexican authorities warned as the migrants approached that only travelers with valid documents and visas, or with claims for asylum or other forms of protection, would be allowed into Mexico. They threatened deportation for those who tried to enter illegally and said they would process the migrants one by one.

But on Friday morning, thousands tried to cross the border en masse, surging past Guatemalan border guards *before being turned back by a contingent of unarmed Mexican riot police officers.*

Officials said that as of late Sunday, they had received more than 1,000 asylum requests from caravan members at the border. Some migrants were taken to a local fairground that had been converted into a temporary government shelter. Many others remained on a bridge spanning the Suchiate River, waiting to be processed by Mexican officials.

Officials also said that some migrants might be eligible for humanitarian visas, or even for safe-passage permits that would allow them to travel to the northern border of Mexico and apply for protection in the United States. In response to another migrant caravan last spring, Mexican officials distributed hundreds of safe-passage permits to participants.

The revived caravan started moving on foot toward Tapachula about 5 a.m. on Sunday, and the procession was orderly and peaceful. Some Mexican residents along the road cheered for the group or handed out bananas, tortillas and water.

Several hours into their journey, Francisco Echevarria, a top federal migration official in the state of Chiapas, appeared in a police pickup truck and urged the migrants to register at a shelter.

When the migrants demanded proof that they would not be deported if they did so, Mr. Echevarria offered to take several to the shelter to show that the rumors were false, and to begin their asylum processes. About 10 of the migrants took him up on his offer and hopped in the back of the truck.

Among the people in the procession was Juan Carlos García García, 16, from Honduras, where he had been a laborer in the coffee fields.

"It's not a crime to migrate," he said as he marched north. "We've not done anything against Mexican law."

He added: "They said they weren't going to allow us to pass. But God has the last word."

To this day, no one can say with any degree of certainty what the exact number of illegal immigrants looking for a better standard of living have actually entered the US. One day, the number is reported to be 11 million, then, not too long after that a subsequent report comes out projecting the number to be twice that amount. No one really knows, and because they don't know, it's just easier for most people in the US to simply go about their daily lives and ignore all the possible impacts the ever-increasing immigrant population is having, and is going to have, on the US economy for generations to come.

In fact, by the year 2044, it is projected that the White non-Hispanic population in the US will no longer be the majority race/ethnic group when compared to all other minorities; and within 16 short years after that, by the year 2060, it is expected that no individual race or ethnic group in the US will have a majority as the minority population rises to 56 percent of the total population, an increase of almost 50 percent from current census numbers today. But, what's most concerning about these estimates, or projections, is the fact they are based on current day data and they do not take into account the adverse effects of all the other known and unknown socioeconomic uprisings facing struggling countries throughout the world.

In an April 20, 2012 article in *Gallup*, written by Jon Clifton, polling showed that approximately 13 percent of the world's adults (more than 640 million people) claim they would like to leave their country permanently. Of those 640 million or so, 150 million would like to come to the US, mostly from China, Nigeria, and India.

Are you keeping up with the math here, especially when you add children into the data?

As the White non-Hispanic population continues to decrease relative to the immigrant population, it is very likely that the Hispanic/Latin population in the US, with their current size, anticipated growth rate, and unwavering commitment to make the US their new home, could easily become the single largest race/ethnic group by the year 2100, if not before. And because of this, English as the primary language in the US could easily become the second language to a predominantly Spanish speaking population.

If you are finding all this hard to believe, I call your attention to the Miami area, which today is considered a microcosm of what the US is going to become over the vast majority of the country as the twenty-second century rolls around.

THE TRANSFORMATION OF A TRILLION DOLLAR INDUSTRY

Time for a Mental Note

Taco Bell employee fired for refusing to serve English-speaking customer

By Louis Casiano | ***Fox News***

A Spanish-speaking Taco Bell employee in Florida was let go by the fast food chain after a video circulating on social media this week showed her refusing to serve an English-speaking customer.

The video shows the employee at the restaurant's Hialeah location appearing to become annoyed when customer Alexandria Montgomery tried placing her order in English, the Miami Herald reported.

After getting nowhere, Montgomery asks to speak with a manager.

The employee, who identifies herself in the video as Luisa, replies in Spanish: "She is in her house sleeping," in a dismissive tone before saying "Honey, I have a car behind you," and closing the window.

She then threatens to call the police.

"Can you move, please? I have an order behind you," she says. "There is no one who speaks English. This is Hialeah, I'm sorry."

Hialeah is located north of Miami International Airport and is predominantly Latino.

"I'm trying to order and she's telling me I can't order because she doesn't speak English. Who's wrong?," Montgomery responded.

The video shows two other Taco Bell employees coming to the drive-thru window, but neither helps Montgomery place her order.

The customer ultimately leaves without making a purchase. No other employees in the restaurant at the time spoke English, the employee said.

"This incident happened Wednesday night around 10:30 p.m.," Montgomery told El Nuevo Herald. "I contacted the manager and after explaining to her what happened all she did was apologize and say 'thank you,' and the call was disconnected."

In a statement, Taco Bell said, "This individual no longer works for the brand."

A spokesperson told the EL Nuevo Herald that "this does not meet our customer service expectations" and "We have worked quickly to resolve with the customer to ensure this doesn't happen again

Montgomery's Facebook post garnered over 4,000 comments as of Friday. Most were in support of her.

"Hialeah is still part of Florida and, as far as I remember, correct me if I'm wrong, Florida is part of the UNITED STATES OF AMERICA, it's a country where English is the language we speak. This is a shame for the Hispanic / Latino community," commented a Facebook user.

I'm sorry here in America we speak English! You can speak any kind of language you want but if you want to live here, I'd expect you to at least learn our language," another wrote.

According to the 2010 census, around 89 percent of Hialeah residents speak Spanish as their first or second language and more than 94 percent identify as Hispanic or Latino.

For reasons that can be explained, but most in power today don't want to verbalize for fear of backlash or being labeled a certain type of person, there is a relatively quiet and mostly ignored immigrant invasion occurring to the demographics of the US population.

An invasion that shows no signs of ever stopping and will continue so long as (a) politicians remain concerned more with holding onto their political party's power as opposed to focusing on what's best for the country, and (b) younger generations unwittingly become tolerant and amenable to the negative effects of a more socially diversified culture. As result, it is very likely that the US as a whole will unintentionally lose a large portion of its Anglo-Saxon heritage by the turn of the twenty-second century.

Generational Partnering: Building a Better Tomorrow for Everyone

By the year 2030, it is estimated that at least half of the working class in the US will be self-employed without employer benefits and little to no savings to fall back on in case of an emergency or use for retirement. In fact, a study reported in 2016 showed 56 percent of Americans had less than $10,000 saved for retirement, and one in three had no savings at all for retirement. Adding to this problem is $4 trillion in consumer debt that continues to reach new highs year in and year out. Statistics that are very alarming to say the least.

Over the next two decades a sobering phenomenon will be emerging throughout the US economy. Business failures in the US will reach unprecedented levels as (a) inexperienced and under-funded retirees startup small businesses to try and offset shortfalls in their retirement accounts; (b) inexperienced and underfunded members of Generations X, Y, and Z, frustrated with not finding a suitable job that is an extension of their personality, startup small businesses in the hope trying to make it on their own; (c) the next generation of business owners, executives, and entrepreneurs struggle to find a competitive edge as they continue to compete on price and not "value" while ignoring demographic shifts happening all around them; (d) federal, state, and local debt structures become so large and unsustainable that higher taxes will need to be raised starting with businesses; and (e) forward thinking and progressive tech base companies take control over, and subsequently push out of the market, what used to be "bricks and mortar" small businesses.

If you think the future is bright for the US economy, think again. There is a huge conundrum afoot and no one seems to know what to do about it.

Today, we have a country with over half of its population age fifty-five and over with an inadequate amount of funds saved up for their retirement years. A country that also has roughly 28 percent of its total working population with absolutely no retirement savings at all, compounded by the fact that people are living longer due to an enhanced focus on quality of life and medical advancements. To be perfectly frank, by the time 2030 rolls around, when most, if not all, Baby Boomers in the US should have retired, more than half will not be financially able to.

What this also means by the year 2030 is that besides the US Social Security Administration being under a tremendous amount of stress to provide retirees with their statutory funds, other government sponsored social programs will come under enormous pressure to continue funding long standing entitlement programs that so many millions of people rely on from one month to the next. If there was ever a worse-case scenario for the US economy when it comes to providing for its elderly and underprivileged, the decade of 2030 will see it all unfold if corrective measures aren't implemented soon.

As much as I would love to rail on the ineffectiveness of most elected officials, I would much rather spend time productively trying to help minimize any undue stress or hardship about to be applied to an aging US population over the next decade. I would also like to try and give some assistance to the younger generations looking to find their niche in life. Both attempts, starting with something called the "abundance mentality."

The "abundance mentality" requires individuals to have a long-term view of mankind and human based events. A thought process if you will that is re-enforced by the fact that there's plenty of resources, opportunities, and successes to spread around for all participant who are willing to work for it, and, get along with one another in a fair and reasonable manner. Needless to say, most progressive business owners, executives, and entrepreneurs have this particular mentality.

In order to address this issue we need to break the discussion down into two approaches: (a) those seeking employment and (b) those seeking to become business owners.

Luckily for all generations wanting to work in the US, the economy has been on an upward trend for quite some time; and although political and/or economic trends could change things in the coming years, no one is predicting a catastrophic event that would alter the numerous opportunities found within the US job market. In fact, as of August 2018, it was reported that there were over 7 million job openings and 6.2 million unemployed. Great news, right? Not so fast. If you haven't noticed there is a culture war raging in the US, and there are no signs it will be ending any time soon.

On one side of the argument, you have employers who claim they are desperately looking for qualified applicants to fill numerous positions within their organizations. And although a large number of these positions require training in order to move skills from a paper-based "bricks and mortar" society to one that is more recently tech and automated based, employers have not been that willing to spend the necessary dollars on advancing the skill levels of employees once they've been hired.

For the other side of the argument, you will find it interesting that candidates looking for employment have become more particular in choosing the jobs they want even though they are more than qualified for the position. Their hesitations of late is centered around the fact the that wages and salaries being offered by employers are no longer adequate and need to be raised, which is fine so long as the economy stays strong and competition for particular job placements remain high.

Time for a Mental Note

In a recent article posted online by the *Chicago Tribune* entitled: "There are 7 million unemployed and 6.2 million job openings.

What's the problem?" The *Washington Post* writer, Heather Long, composes a very telling look at just how the US job market is actually performing.

> *The United States has a record 6.2 million job openings. It's the highest number since the Labor Department began tracking job postings in 2000.*
>
> *At the same time, there are 7 million unemployed Americans. That's almost one job for every person searching for a role. This should be a no-brainer, right? Get the jobless onto the doorsteps of these employers.*
>
> *Sadly, it's not that easy. There are two fundamental problems with the job market today: Businesses complain they can't find qualified workers to fill the jobs, and workers complain they aren't getting paid enough.*
>
> *The view from a lot of CEOs is that there aren't any good workers left. Over half of small business owners in America say there are "few or no qualified applicants" for the jobs they have open right now, according to the latest NFIB Small Business Survey released hours before the Labor Department said there was a record number of job openings. We have heard for years that there aren't enough computer programmers, but the grumbling goes deeper than that.*
>
> *Too many workers these days show up drunk or high on weed, managers say. Or they refuse to work late or on weekends. As The Washington Post's Chico Harlan reported over the weekend, some companies are bringing in robots because they can't find enough humans willing to do the work anymore. The other obvious solution is to bring in more immigrants, but President Trump wants to do the exact opposite.*

Last week, he proposed slashing legal immigration by 50 percent in the next decade.

"The demand for qualified warm bodies remains healthy but the supply of them remains stunted," says Peter Boockvar, chief market analyst at The Lindsey Group in Virginia. He points out that over 18 percent of Americans between the ages of 25 and 54 aren't working. That's almost one in five people in that "prime age" category. It wasn't like that in the boom times of the 1990s and early 2000s. There would be about 2.5 million more prime age workers employed today if the same percentage of Americans were working now as in the 1990s.

But workers also have a message for CEOs: Pay us more. Wages are barely growing. Companies have to pay up if they want better talent. During the Great Recession, there were almost 7 unemployed people for every job opening. Businesses could afford to be choosy—and offer low salaries. Today, the situation is dramatically different. There's only 1 job seeker for every opening. Experts keep forecasting that wages will rise. This kind of "tight labor market" should trigger fatter paychecks for workers, but so far, that isn't happening.

"When businesses give this anecdotal evidence that they can't find the workers they want, the first thing I would ask them is: Have you increased your pay?" says economist Elise Gould of the Economic Policy Institute, a liberal think tank.

It's telling that 5 of the 10 jobs the U.S. government projects will grow the fastest over the next decade pay less than $25,000 a year. The jobs have titles such as personal care aid, home health aid and food preparer. It's a vicious cycle: Companies don't pay enough. Then they complain workers aren't dedicated and loyal.

Gould's advice to businesses is to "be a less picky" and, in some cases, to stop discriminating. She notes that the <u>unemployment rate</u> for black workers (7.3 percent) is still much higher than for whites (3.7 percent). There are people ready to work. The Washington Post's Jennifer Contrera followed Donna Maria Osborne, a 59-year-old African-American woman in Washington D.C., to a recent job fair. Despite years of experience as an administrative assistant, she was routinely told she wasn't what employers were looking for. "I think it's my age," she says.

In one particularly telling moment, Osborne finds a booth at the job fair that's trying to hire people for a call center. Osborne feels like this is it, until the representative explains, "They are looking for a background in call centers. Billing, and so forth. So if you worked in a doctor's office or something like that, that's customer service, but it wouldn't be on the scale of this call center environment."

The company won't hire Osborne because she hasn't worked in a call center before. It sounds mind-boggling, but some employers are still that picky. They refuse to even do minimal training. At the same time, Trump's first budget proposes cutting government-funded job training programs by 40 percent.

An environment like this—low unemployment, lots of jobs openings—should be win for workers. Salaries should be rising and employers should be willing to give people a chance. But that's not what is happening. Instead, CEOs are frustrated they can't fill jobs, workers are upset their pay is meager and millions of job seekers just want someone to give them a chance.

Trump talks about wanting to create 25 million new jobs. The issue isn't the job openings. America keeps breaking new records for job openings. It's been like that for over a year. The issue is training people for jobs—and paying them more. It's proving a lot harder to solve those problems."

But you know what, I'm not convinced that either of these arguments hold all the water employers and candidates would like for everyone to believe. The reality is, generational "values" are colliding like never before and will continue to do so until for at least the next two decades. Why? Because the filters being used by individuals from all generations are getting overrun by emotions clogging any hope of logical outcomes to prevail.

Let's face it, regardless of what generation anyone comes from, we have all developed a "value" system based on gender, race, age, and religion that automatically creates prejudices. Prejudices that determine whether or not we'll accept something or someone. There is simply no getting around it.

Take the older generations for example, GI and Silent. These are generations who are more conservative, politically active, and not afraid to tell people what they're thinking; and therefore, hold a much different "value" system than the Baby Boomers and Generations X and Y.

Then came the Baby Boomers who outright revolted against the social norms embraced by their parents and grandparents. Boomers openly moved toward sexual promiscuity, rampant drug use, rock and roll music, flamboyant cloth, and outlandish hairstyles, not to mention squandering way over $7 trillion worth of savings left behind by the two previous generations before them.

As for Generations X and Y, they come to the forefront with similar "values" (as was the case with the GI and Silent Generations back in the day), full of a sense of entitlement and narcissism. They live everything hi-tech, spending endless hours hunkered down and consumed with electronic gadgets, software, and applications, and appear more tolerant and less bigoted than previous generations.

Now comes Generation Z, a generation that will more than likely change the entire world for ever as they digitally bond with technology like no previous generation before them. Using creativity and innovation to make the world smaller, more efficient, and self-reliant.

Predictions indicate that Generation Z's "value" system will be based on a similar foundation to that of Generation X and Y's, however, Generation Z is quickly emerging to become the most culturally and ethnically diverse generation every to occupy US soil. Although technically more savvy and advanced than their parents and grandparent, Generation Z appears to be more risk adverse, independent, and less likely to believe there truly does exist an American dream of owning a home with two cars and having an average number of kids. And here's probably the most crucial thing for future business owners, executives, and entrepreneurs to understand about Generation Z, and that is they will expect to find jobs that are an expression of their identity; which by all accounts today is going to be a serious problem until such time that employers and candidates find some common ground in which to exist together, or, less tolerant business owners, executives, and entrepreneurs are no longer in charge of the hiring practices.

In the meantime, though, regardless of which generation a candidate is from, finding a job that fits into specific lifestyle parameter is going to be a challenge. As industries continue to move away from "bricks and mortar" operations, and more toward tech-based, employers will eventually have to come to a decision whether to pay aging candidates a lower wage, initially, with the thought in mind that additional training might be required in the future as a means to increase skill level, knowing they are more likelier than not to be responsible, loyal, and on-time each day; or, pay an initial higher wage to younger more skilled employees who have a tendency not to stick around for very long once word gets out that a higher paying job just became available. A dilemma that will be playing out for a decade to come.

But here's a unique thought for all generations to consider, what about the independent minded retirees and younger generations who see ownership as their destiny. Should there exist a generational partnership in order to bridge the gaps between their "value" systems?

Answer: Absolutely, and here's how.

Stop for a minute and think about all the experience and wisdom age affords you as you get older. Not necessarily from an actual occupational skill level capacity, although that could become a very useful commodity at some point, but rather from a life's skills perspective in general.

As we have all learned over the years, wouldn't have been great to have a nonjudgmental, compassionate, loyalist available at a moment's notice to provide sound guidance when a decision was about to affect the outcome of something. No question!

I am convinced more so than ever that if generations of all stripes could find a pathway to work together in a transparent and equitable manner, great things could happen beyond the wildest dreams of everyone involved. Older generations have their role to play as well as the younger generations; and so long as everyone understands their individual role, synergy, automatically takes over to where a solid foundation is cast for future operations to be built upon. Eventually, the older generations will fade away leaving behind their trusted younger generation to carry on until it's their turn one day to once again link up with a partner in order to perpetuate the business.

This all may sound Pollyannaish to some, but I can assure you the reality of such a paradigm far outweighs any alternative that is being espoused today in the halls of academia or on Wall Street. Developing a business purpose that spans multiple generations may not be that unique in the business world, however, the mere fact that members from different generations can come together for the betterment of each other's future creates "value" on so many levels. A "value" that can be recognized by both business owners and customers alike.

Whether these generational partnerships are through joint ventures or strategic alliances with one another, it really doesn't matter. What truly matters is the actual coming together of diverse entities and/or individuals as a solution for meeting the future demands of customers in a way that creates "value," satisfaction, and loyalty.

The Four Year Plan: College vs. Trade School

If entrepreneurs like Bill Gates, Steve Jobs, Mark Zuckerberg, and Henry Ford have taught the business world anything, you don't need a college education in order to be successful at an occupation you enjoy and have a passion for.

Most everyone reading this book knows that within four to five years of graduating from a high school curriculum, a student can obtain any number of degrees from higher education. Within seven years of graduating from a high school curriculum career minded professionals can become doctors, lawyers, and/or acquire master degrees in a variety of educational disciplines. Granted, most students are required to pay for such education, but nonetheless, they come away with a piece of paper that states they have achieved a certain level of expertise in a given field of study.

Did you also know that within four to five years of graduating from a high school curriculum individuals willing to learn trade or craft can become certified to perform certain tasks that require a particular level of expertise? And within approximately seven years' time of graduating from a high school curriculum highly skilled tradesman, a.k.a., craftsmen, could acquire enough expertise to become highly successful business owner, executives, or entrepreneur in the field of construction.

Now you have to ask yourself, what's the major differences between the two career paths?

1. When going to college or seeking a higher education most students have to pay their way through the entire process. Going into a trade or craft, employers immediately pay the student, i.e., apprentice, to learn while on the job.

2. For college students to graduate within four to five years, they would theoretically have to be full-time students, leaving little spare time for any other activity. This would also mean that they would be almost totally dependent on others, financially, to provide for their food, lodging, tuition, books, transportation, and insurances such as medical, dental, vision, auto, and life.

3. For individuals going into a trade or craft, and given the fact they are reasonably compensated from practically the very beginning, they are able to gain life skills earlier than students going to college would be able to. Life skills that inherently come from being able to provide for themselves financially.

4. In a number of instances, college and higher education bound students, along with their parents and in some cases their grandparents, are required to takeout student loans to help pay for their educational experience. These are typically low interest loans that will eventually need to be paid back in full whether a student graduates or not.

5. Learning a trade or craft usually requires an individual to perform acts of physical labor in most any external environment. College students are more often than not either attending school sitting in a classroom environment or online in the comfort of their home.

In an August 8, 2012, *Forbes* article written by John Ebersole entitled, "Why a College Degree?" it reads in part:

> *The median cost of a four-year degree in-state at a public institution is about $16,000 per year, or $64,000 overall... What does a $64,000 investment return in dividends? According to the Bureau of Labor Statistics, not only is there a $400 per week difference in earnings between those with a high school diploma and those with a bachelor's degree, there is also a substantial difference in unemployment. As of the end of 2011, high-school only workers were unemployed at a rate of 9.4% while those with a bachelor's degree had an unemployment rate of 4.9% (4.1% as of July 2012). Most interesting is the fact that the total cost of degree acquisition ($64,000) is repaid through the increased, salary ($1600 per month, or $19,200 per year) in less than four years. Not a bad ROI, and with a 50% increase in job security to boot. The difference between a degree holder's earnings and those of a high school-only worker are sizeable over a lifetime. According to the U.S. Government Info Web site, "...a high school graduate can expect, on average, to earn $1.2 million; those with a bachelor's degree $2.1 million; and people with a master's degree $2.5 million.*

Anyone reading this article in Forbes would instantly come away with the notion that it's a must for high school graduates to go onto college if they want to seek their fame and fortune because it's the only path for career minded people to avoid being relegated to menial tasks all their life. But I can assure that is a misleading and wrong supposition to come away with. And here's why!

I grant you that if individuals stop improving their available skill level after high school they will be very limited when it comes to choosing a career path that will potentially lead to earning higher levels of income. However, this does not hold true for individuals willing to put in the effort to learn a trade or craft after high school. In fact, I would argue that given the entire time continuum of earning a living and acquiring the necessary life skills that will help an individual avoid serious financial risks in the future, the sooner a person can be self-sufficient in life the better able he or she will be to cope with adverse and potentially life-changing events down the road.

In a September 14, 1998, article written in *ENR* by Ray J. Carrara, Mr. Carrara stated that:

> *Since the 1950s the need for employees with a college degree has remained static at about 20% of the working population, and yet we prepare more than 50% of our youth to pursue a traditional college degree today. In the '50s, the need for skilled workers hovered around 15%. The remaining 65% of jobs were in unskilled areas... Today, the need for technically skilled employees is approaching 60% of the workforce and is expected to rise to 77% by the year 2005. These technical jobs do not require a college degree. By pushing the college route, we are preparing 50 to 60% of our youth to compete for 20% of future jobs.*

To simply say, imply, or try to document why, that high school graduates absolutely need to have a college education as a prerequisite to entering the workforce and securing a good paying job is not only wrong but disingenuous to students trying to choose a career path, but it's also wrong and disingenuous to the parents and grandparents who feel obligated to spend the money for a misconceived notion that could severely impact their standard of living as they move into their retirement years.

There is a great book that I would highly recommend for parents, grandparents, and students for that matter, who have young adult children trying to make a choice between numerous career paths. The book is called *Rich Dad Poor Dad* written by Robert Kiyosaki. It's a personal finance book that has been translated into fifty-one different languages and has sold over 27 million copies worldwide.

In the book, Mr. Kiyosaki discusses the importance, or lack thereof, of finishing an education to the satisfaction of others—a question also raised by other notable self-help advocates like Dave Ramsey, who has authored a number of books, most notably, *The Total Money Makeover: A Proven Plan for Financial Fitness*.

For years, all Mr. Kiyosaki heard from his father was that he needed to go to a good school so he could land a good job and be successful in life, as if school was the only career path one could take to find a decent salary and job security. But as Mr. Kiyosaki describes in his book, going to a good school truly doesn't equal success in life.

As Mr. Kiyosaki points out in his book, most parents and grandparent today, like his father, think that a good school will help their children avoid these pitfalls of life. But unfortunately for them, their hopeful wishes of children and grandchildren someday becoming a doctors, lawyers, or high-ranking executive will in no way make them financially free in the purest sense.

Time for Mental Note

According to LIMRA, a worldwide research, learning, and development organization and source of industry information for over 850 financial services firms based in Windsor, CT, they concluded that in 1989, less than 1 percent of retirees had educational loans. By 2013, that percentage had risen to 15 percent. LIMRA's data indicated that both parents and grandparents are acquiring more and more student loan debt to help their children and grandchildren.

In a June 2016 article in *The College Fix* entitled "Nearly 64 percent of jobs don't require college education, but wait—there's more" it references that the Bureau of Labor Statistics reported that only about one-third of all jobs required an education beyond a high school level. It also alarmingly noted that the amount of student loan debt had risen to an unbelievable $1.2 trillion.

According to the US Census, about one-third of all Americans have a bachelor's degree, however, as just mentioned in the article, the Bureau of Labor Statistics indicates that only about one-third of all jobs require an education beyond high school. So if only one-third of the available jobs in America require a post-high school education, why are so many families and/or students willing to go into debt pursing degrees they will never use when two-thirds of the available jobs in America are waiting to be filled by people who want to work and make a living?

Short answer: A not-too-distant memory by earlier generations of parents and grandparents. I know; I'm a Baby Boomer.

With the thought of the Great Depression still fresh in their minds, all parents and grandparents of the Baby Boomer Generation ever wanted for their children and grandchildren was for them to have a good education and a secure future. The mere thought of their children and grandchildren toiling at menial jobs, scraping by trying to make ends meet, being underemployed, earning low wages, and paying higher taxes was something they were not willing to tolerate if they didn't have to. As a result, today we have legacies of future generations wanting the same opportunity to attend institutions of higher learning, especially now with all the alluring things being created by and through technology.

Time for a Mental Note

"We are lending money we don't have to kids who can't pay it back to train them for jobs that no longer exist. That's nuts." (Mike Rowe)

In years past, it has always been an interesting phenomenon to me to hear business owners, executives, and entrepreneurs express their views on the educational and/or training value of their potential managers, supervisors, and employees in general. Some business owners argue that an employee having come up through the ranks of an industry trade program provides the most value to a service-based company, long-term, because of the knowledge gained through hands on field or shop experience; while other business owners, executives, and entrepreneurs of service-based companies feel that employees having a college education provides for a broader sense of business and procedural acumen that will accelerated a potential employees advancement up the chain of command, which in turn provides for both an inherent short-term and long-term benefit to the company. So which philosophy is correct?

Answer: Neither.

The reality is, a person's knowledge about a particular subject can only be gained through one's *desire* to learn. Just because an individual has hands on knowledge gained through experiences in a field or shop environment doesn't necessarily give him or her a leg up over someone in the same profession who just graduated from college, and vice versa. In order for people to become sustainable, successful, wealthy, and secure in life, some amount of education and/or knowledgeable based experience is required. But even then, unless an individual is self-employed, most jobs on earth are not guaranteed for life.

If we want to face facts head on, we have to be realistic and acknowledge that the days of individuals having a thirty- or forty-year career at one job or having one occupation is going to become increasing limited over the next fifty years. More than anything, advancements in technology will see to it.

But what I've learned over the years, contrary to popular belief, people looking to climb the corporate ladder do not need to have a college education, nor, do they need to have an extensive amount of field or shop experience, in order to be a highly successful business owner, executive, manager, or supervisor is a service-based business. College is not for everyone, nor is everyone meant to work with their hands in a field or shop environment. Success in any profession is based solely on one's *desire* to succeed.

Background: St. Joseph, MO

The year was roughly 1910 when a group of immigrants from Austria-Hungary bravely made their trek across Europe and boarded a ship in pursuit of a new life in America. Part of the group included my four-year-old grandfather, his mother, and two siblings.

After making it to America and unable to speak any English at the time, my great grandmother set out to lead her family with very meager means in tow across the country, settling in a small town located on the Missouri River, where they would eventually be reunited once again with my great grandfather who had come to America ahead of them in order to prepare for their new life together.

As my grandfather grew up, he was not much different than the other immigrant children in the neighborhood. He and his siblings went to school where they learned to speak English, working odd jobs to help support the family, while others in the family tended to small gardens where they grew vegetables and produced enough grapes to satisfy their annual consumption of homemade wine.

After graduating from high school my grandfather took a job at the local Burlington Railroad yard where he spent most of his day cleaning the boiler compartment of steam engines. Although an extremely dirty and somewhat hazardous job due to the inhalation of all the soot and ash that became airborne, my grandfather laboriously did his job while constantly dreaming of a much better life outside the boiler compartments of steam engines.

Fascinated with AC and DC power, and its effects on motors and appliances, my grandfather started spending as much time as he could tinkering with old motors and learning as much as he could about how they actually worked. Eventually, his passion took him to night school where he learned how to repair radios, rewind motors, and eventually repair appliances.

Confident that he had eventually gained the necessary knowledge he needed to get into the world of electricity and electrical/electronic repair, my grandfather landed his first part-time job working for a small electrical company in the area. At which point, he said good-bye to the Burlington Railroad yard and all their soot and ash filled engine compartments needing to be cleaned.

With each new electrical assignment, my grandfather would sling his heavy leather bag full of tools over one shoulder while carrying bags of material in both hands as he traveled to and from each location via the local streetcar system. It was a profession my grandfather enjoyed doing and one he felt confident would lead him to a much better life some day

By this time, my grandfather's family, most still living together and caring for one another, had moved to a much larger home where accommodations weren't as crowded and the small garage out back proved to be the perfect location for my grandfather to start a business repairing radios, appliances, and rewinding motors for customers. Then, a few years later, in 1934, my grandfather met the girl of his dreams and married her.

A strong farm girl from Oklahoma, my grandmother was no one to mess around with. At six-foot tall, she was the star player on a ladies basketball association team that toured the region competing in various tournaments. By all accounts, my grandmother was not only tough minded and a great athlete, but she also had a good head on her shoulders when it came to business and management.

As the country continued to sink deeper into the Great Depression, money became extremely tight for most everyone in their town. Often times my grandfather would leave for a service call in the early morning hours and return home later that day with a single chicken to show for his payment. Times were that tough.

Wanting to start their own family even in tough times, my grandparents had two boys roughly eighteen months apart over the next six years. Then came the World War II as the Japanese bombed the US Pacific Fleet at Pearl Harbor.

With America now fully engage in war, the need to rebuild the Pacific Fleet became critical for the country's defense as the fear of Japan preparing to strike the continental US loomed greater. Needless to say, it was an extremely stressful time for all Americans as families struggled to get through the aftermath of the Great Depression and prepared to send their sons off to war in a foreign lands across the sea.

As the need for raw materials increased exponentially to support the war effort, certain construction materials became less accessible and more expensive to buy and resell. Copper, the primary source of conducting material used by the electrical industry, just happened to be one of those raw materials in high demand. And without access to copper, the electrical industry struggled.

Without access to copper cable and wire, and feeling a strong sense of patriotism, my grandparents decided to temporarily shut down their small electrical service company, packed up their two young boys, and make the roughly 1,700-mile journey to the Mare Island Naval Ship Yards in northern California. It was there, that my grandfather took an electricians position building and repairing ships for war, and where my grandmother took in boarders for extra income.

As the war started to come to a close, and after seven years of living and working in the northern California ship yard area, my grandparents decided it was time to pack back up and return to their small electrical business back in the Midwest working out of the family garage.

In 1949, as their electrical business continued to grow and prosper, my grandparents moved to an actual business location that also doubled as their home with a large apartment area above the office and garage. With my grandfather spending most of his week servicing customers by day, and estimating projects by night, my grandmother pulled her fair share of the daily duties by caring for the two boys, managing the office, and taking care of the apartment.

Then in 1953, and right out of high school, my father joined the company as an apprentice electrician making $.50/hr. Three short years later, it was uncle's turn to also became an apprentice electrician and start his career shortly after graduating from high school. In the purest sense, my grandparents created what truly became a family business.

Over the next twenty years or so, the family business grew to become one of the leading electrical contractors in a metropolitan area that serviced a regional population of over 150,000. Not only was the family name known for its quality of service for miles around, but customers actually preferred giving their business to my family's family owned business as opposed to other equally qualified competitors in the area.

Time for a Mental Note

For as long as I can remember, my grandfather constantly preached to his family and grandchildren his philosophy for doing business. A philosophy that states, *"Be honest, be humble, be patient, and work hard."* And to this very day, I can still remember hearing him tell my brothers and me about these four characteristics every time someone would ask him about managing the business.

In 1975, both my grandparents had since retired after almost a half a century at the helm of what many would consider a highly successful business. In addition to them building a dominant and respected company, my grandparents also raised two high-quality boys who helped contribute to the families' success story as well as producing nine grandchildren for them, some of which were coming of age and having to make their own career decisions by this time.

Looking to the future and their eventual retirement someday, my dad and uncle struck up a discussion about how the next generation of kids would contribute to the legacy of the family business. From that discussion, each brother decide the path of their own children when it came to being part of the family business. My father gave my brothers, sister, and me one of two options: (a) graduate from college with a four year degree or (b) complete a four-year apprenticeship program through the local IBEW union. That was it, no other options would ever be discussed.

As of today, six out of nine grandchildren joined the company, while the other three pursued successful careers outside the family business. Of the six who eventually joined the construction contracting industry at some point, one came up through the trade as an electrician, while the other five went on to gain their four year and/or post graduate degrees. But even more interesting and impressive, of the five, four went on to study and receive a "masters" electrical license, three of whom had college degrees.

To perform at the highest possible level in business, business owners, executives, entrepreneurs, managers, and supervisors must possess a knowledge about operational processes which are tailored specifically to the requirements of the position being filled. In other words, it doesn't matter where an employee or individual starts a career; it's the journey that gets an employee or individual to their final destination that is critical for one's success to be recognized

The debate between who is more knowledgeable, wise, and valuable, the learned scholar or the tradesman, dates back to the 5th century when the great scholar and philosopher, Socrates, provided his thoughts on *ignorance, knowledge*, and *wisdom*, also known as the learning cycle.

Viewed as one of the most influential scholars and philosophers of his time, Socrates knew his knowledge on various subjects was limited. A compulsive thinker and pursuer of knowledge and wisdom, Socrates routinely questioned those who presented themselves as being the wiser. Wiser in the sense that one may know more than others about how human beings live and go about their daily lives.

Time for a Mental Note

"Awareness of ignorance is the beginning of wisdom." (Socrates)

Throughout his learned studies of humans and their ways, Socrates found that a category of men referred to as "artisans," i.e., craftsmen of that era, along with learned scholars, who indeed did understand certain things that Socrates didn't, took it upon themselves to extend their so-called wisdom in an arrogant manner to think, if not imagine, that they knew more than they actually did. This led Socrates to conclude that all professionals, i.e., scholars, and tradesmen fall prey to this foolish behavior of one knowing more than another, and concluded that it's better for humans to seek and live their own knowledge about how to live as a means to better understand things for themselves as opposed to listening to the hyperbole of others.

In referencing Socrates, when it comes to this century's old argument about which category of individual, learned scholar or tradesman, has more value to a business, I find it interesting that the argument lives on even to this day as business owners still behave in a very similar manner to those artisans and scholars of Socrates's era. Business owners blinded by their own arrogance, prejudices, and paradigms to the valuable knowledge, experience, and contributions of others. And much like the artisans and scholars of Socrates time, these same business owners limit themselves to the potential of hiring valuable employees who could easily help them effectively lead their organizations into the next generational cycle.

As much as some small to mid-sized business owners hate to admit it, they don't necessarily view their operations as business entities. Instead, these types of service-based business owners continue to embrace the timeless reference of owning a "shop," much like business owners did at the turn of the twentieth century when customers would bring their furniture, appliances, radios, motors, sheet metal and plumbing concerns to be repaired. And because of this time honored mind-set, certain small to mid-sized business owners still continue to place a higher value on an employee's technical and skill ability than anything else. Hence, the reason why so many small to midsized business owners look to hiring trade trained employees before those with a college education.

As for the larger, more sophisticated business owners and executive, including those associated with performance based companies, they view their operations in a much different light; which is also why they don't necessarily have a preference on where an employee's background and/or experience originates from. Larger, more sophisticate business owners and executives view their operations more in the light of an actual business entity that not only provides customers with hands-on service, but one that also provides customers with an expanded service offering that in turn creates additional opportunities to grow future revenues.

Let me give you an example of what I'm referring to when it comes to how certain size companies view their own capabilities, especially when you incorporate the concept of risk into the discussion.

Background: Tampa, FL

As the senior project manager for a large out-of-state electrical contractor on a number of large projects, a contractor that would definitely qualified as a *"high performance"* company, it was imperative for our company as part of our risk analysis assessment to partner up with small to medium sized local contractors in the area who shared our principles for conducting business. In doing so, we were extremely fortunate to find one in particular.

The small contractor was owned by an interesting gentleman who started out his career as a tradesman, i.e., electrician, who worked his way up through the ranks as a foreman, general foreman, superintendent, project manager/estimator, and executive. He was the type of person who would literally give you the shirt off his back if you were ever in need of it. In fact, even if you weren't in need of it but expressed some sentimental interest in it, the owner would more than likely just give it to you anyway. He was a true success story who worked every day to provide a comfortable living for his family, employees, and himself.

As a business owner and entrepreneur, the owner led every aspect of his company by example. By his own actions and words, the owner clearly set the tone of the culture and expected attitude of every employee representing his company. A culture that was steeped in employees being calm, pleasant, reasonable, and respectful toward everyone, especially customers, which in a sense, the large contractor I represented at the time was one of.

Accessible 24-7 to everyone (family, friends, employees, customers, and colleagues), I'm not sure when he had any downtime to himself. In fact, there was never a significant decision made in the company that didn't get his stamp of approval first.

As time passed, and the relationship between our two companies became stronger, there was no question that if another large opportunity, i.e., project, came up in the area the small contractor would be the first contractor we would call for support. And eventually a project did.

As our work together in the area was coming to a close, the large contractor I was working for at the time was offered another very large university lab project that was planned to be built in the downtown area. An area of town less than a ten-minute drive from the small contractor's office.

Excited to team up again, the owner of the small contracting company and I scheduled a meet and greet with the construction manager awarded the project. A meeting by all indication that went extremely well, solidifying either one of our two companies being able to do the project, if not as a team.

Faced with a major decision to make, it was decided by my company's senior management that we would have to pass on the large lab project even though it would have been built with a long time customer company. The reason for this decision was simple. Our risk analysis showed that available resources in the area would not become available in time to handle the large design/built lab project; therefore we weren't willing to take the unnecessary risks.

Informing our local partner of the decision, the owner immediately expressed an interest in pursuing the lab project solo with our customer. So I called the customer to inform them of our internal decision, then offered a solution by recommending our local partner take on the project by themselves with our support, if necessary. As a result of that discussion, and knowing the company I was with would still be involved if necessary, the customer moved forward with involving the owner of the small contractor.

A couple weeks later, the owner of the small contacting company paid me a visit at one of the project sites I was overseeing.

Slowly sitting down in a chair across from me, the owner proceeded to tell me that he had called the customer and walk away from the project. When I asked why, he said after some extensive thought, he had decided that the project did not fit the skill set or core competencies he had personally come to rely on for all his years as an executive and owner. In other words, the owner rightfully knew his limitations given the current organization dynamic of his company, recognizing, that in order to successfully deliver a project of this nature he would need to push his company's operation outside its comfort zone when it came to delivering a reliable service to its customers. A decision, contractors like him, should be commended for.

Time for a Mental Note

"Wisdom is not a product of schooling but of the lifelong attempt to acquire it." (Albert Einstein)

In the story I just told, it is relatively easy to see the difference in mind-sets between that of a larger business and one that is much smaller and service-orientated. Although both are quality businesses governed by good and sound business practices, it's the larger business being the one with the confidence to take on the more challenging opportunities if resources are available.

Time for a Mental Note

Regardless of size, every business needs to be comfortable with not only their own skill sets and core competencies, but the level of risk they are willing to take on at any given time. Skill sets, core competencies, and risk that have nothing to do with data, algorithms, or a software applications I might add.

As the next generation of business owners, executives and entrepreneurs ascend to the chair of control, they have to understand that technology alone will not be able to provide the necessary knowledge required to make the right decision every time. In fact, future decisions will dictate that in order to make the right decision more often than not, personal experiences, knowledge, awareness, and a gut feel will be the prerequisite for all new business owners, executives, and entrepreneurs. Innate things that technology is incapable of helping with.

The reason I bring this up is because I fear the need for personal experience, knowledge, awareness, and gut feel are characteristics that members of Generations X and Y, and soon to be Z, are going to outright dismiss in favor of letting an impersonal technology, enhanced through algorithms, applications, and gadgetry, guide their way via computer screens or digital displays. Business owners, executives, and entrepreneurs of tomorrow have got to understand that human interaction, gained through personal experiences, is essential, and not an option, for short-term survival and long-term sustainability.

CHAPTER

6

Understanding the Risks
of Being a Business Owner:
Now and in the Future

The concept of risk in owning a business, particularly one in the construction industry, might seem to be a simple and straight proposition, but I can assure it's not. In fact, there are plenty of cases in the past where business owners, executives, and entrepreneurs felt reasonably sure that they had adequately performed the necessary due diligence ahead of time before making a critical decision, only to find out later that their decision was dead wrong. Not because they had faulty information to analyze before the decision or commitment was made, but it was because the inherent nature of owning a business where the terrain can change at any given period of time reached up and grabbed them when they least expected it.

Background: Los Angeles, CA

In the mid-1980s, I joined a medium-sized electrical contracting company owned by a very pleasant husband and wife duo. Both in their forties at the time, he came up through the ranks as an electrician, while the wife focused as the primary care giver at home to their two kids, and simultaneously honed her skills at being an office manager. By the time I had arrived, they had established themselves as truly successful contractors in a relatively short period of time working for a handful of trusted general contractors and end-users over the previous ten years or so.

One of the reasons for their success story was due to how well they managed the cash flow needs of the business. Starting from scratch, it became obvious to them at the time that the actual cash flow of the business was in effect their own personal cash flow, expenditures were constantly monitored, billings to customers would always go out in a timely manner, and receivables were constantly tracked in order to keep cash coming into the business. It was pretty clear to all that worked for their company that having to constantly go to the bank for an operating loan was not part of their business model.

Upon arriving in the summer of 1985, the husband and wife contractor duo had just started their new office and warehouse expansion program. As the company and its revenues continued to grow in a seemly healthy manner, it was becoming increasingly evident that the existing facility was quickly becoming too cramped and inefficient to effectively operate and grow the business. Optimism for the future was running very high and I could sense a very positive by most everyone the day I walked in the door for the first time.

But there was another reason for the couple's confidence and optimism running so high, and that was because about nine months prior to my arrival the company had been awarded what appeared to be a very lucrative multimillion dollar time and material (T & M) with a guaranteed maximum value (GMAX) contract for the renovation and expansion of a very high profile historic hotel in downtown Los Angeles. A contract that would effectively double the size of the company's existing revenue; and as a side note, the new contract was also the reason I was hired.

Needing a large contract person to oversee the project, the contractor apparently came to grips with the fact that he, nor his existing management staff, had either the time or expertise to manage the overwhelming nuances and complexities required by the newly acquired contract, factors that should have been strongly considered even before pursuing the project but obviously the distraction of the shining object in front of them blocked all that from view. An occurrence not all that uncommon for contractors who are more focused on short-term successes then the liquidity required to secure long-term sustainability.

Compounding the contractor's concern for wanting to stay involved with the large complex project was the fact that contrary to the company's other customers, who the contractor had always felt comfortable working for in the past, the contractor had no prior experience dealing with this particular customer in case something happened to go awry. But here again, given the prestige that would come from being part of a massive project such as this one, not to mention the unprecedented profit potential to be generated in the coming months, the contractor set aside his concerns for the unknown customer relationship and marched on with the procurement and delivery the project.

In general, the delivery of the renovation project was no small feat from a design and construction perspective. As part of the funding that went into the design and construction of the project, the owner/developer needed to keep the existing hotel operations functioning with limited interruptions to guest services; and with the vast majority of the historic hotel being opened up to design and construction activities, it started to become increasing apparent to the owner/developer after about a year into the project that the combination of funds, construction loan and continuing revenue stream for hotel operations, allocated for the overall project were not going to be adequate.

As part of their financial restructuring plan to mitigate the anticipated shortfall, the owner/developer decided it was in their best interest to renegotiate the contracts with most, if not all, of the T & M subcontractors—primarily the MEP (mechanical, electrical, and plumbing) contractors. Obviously, this was not met with open arms by the MEP contractors. In fact, it didn't take long before resentment to set in, quickly paving the way for scheduling issues that did nothing more that exacerbate the already strained relationships between some of the subcontractors and the managing members of the owner/developer's staff.

There was no question from the MEP subcontractors' perspective that they were being treated unfairly, however, to the owner/developer, and their lender's auditor, it was strictly business. The mind-set of every MEP subcontractor going into the project was to get paid for services rendered in a timely and unencumbered manner for the entire scope of their respective contract. To the owner/developer, and their lender's auditor, the goal was to complete the project at whatever means necessary; and if anyone of the MEP subcontractors were not going to comply with the renegotiations, it was not going to end well for them.

After weeks of back and forth negotiations between the owner/developer and MEP subcontractors, and while work was still progressing at a somewhat subdued pace, adversely effecting to the overall construction schedule, the owner/developer started to lose patience with the MEP subcontractors refusing to renegotiate their contracts. Fueled by the fear of having to pay more in interest against their construction loan, the owner/developer, as a means to increase leverage on the MEP subcontractors, announced that they were immediately withholding previously unpaid and the current month's progress payment applications

Within days of their decision to withhold payment applications, all but one of the MEP subcontractors had agreed to renegotiate their fee arrangements. Unfortunately, the lone MEP holdout was the contractor I went to work for just six months prior to all this coming down.

With over one hundred craftsmen on the project, our exposure was dramatically increasing by the day. Fearful of abandoning the project until the matter got settled, the contractor started to see how the lack of funds coming in from the renovation project was affecting the company's overall ability to pay for its short-term obligations in a timely manner. To make matters worse, now faced with the majority of the company's working capital going to support the large hotel renovation project, financial support of the company's other projects was quickly becoming exhausted to the point where supplement third party financing was inevitable.

Knowing he had to do something, the contractor decided to return a call from an industry consulting firm who had been pursuing him for a number of months in an attempt to sell him their expert consulting services. And given their reputation throughout the construction industry, the contractor felt that if anyone could help him during this very traumatic time it would be them and their depth of resources. So he set up a meet and greet with the consulting firm at everyone's earliest convenience.

Having been asked to attend the meeting, I sat quietly by the contractor's side as he jumped right in without giving the industry consultant much of an opportunity to say anything promotional about his firm's capabilities, and began to methodically lay out all the reasons why he felt his company had gotten itself into the dire financial straits it had with what appeared to be limited options for recovery. He went onto say, given the stellar reputation that preceded the industry consulting firm, it was his high hope that once the industry consultant was able to hear what had transpired on the project to date, that his firm would be able to provide the necessary strategy, guidance, and pathway to resolving the problem.

Somewhat surprised and startled at how the discussion had turned so quickly from an anticipated sales pitch to an actual need for expert services, the industry consultant reluctantly started to take a few notes; interjecting at times with some benign and unassuming questions. It was obvious to me watching this all unfold that the industry consultant was not in any position at that time to provide aid and comfort to contractor.

As the meeting started to wrap up, the industry consultant stated that he would go back to his firm, explain the situation, and return in a couple weeks for a follow up discussion. But in the meantime, though, he would send along the necessary engagement documents to the contractor for review and signature. In other words, the guidance wasn't going to come free of charge.

Feeling a sense of relief, the contractor was convinced that the industry consultant would surely return in a couple weeks with a "silver bullet" to cure his financial woes, and why not? Prior to the meeting, the industry consultant had been telling the contractor for quite some time about all the great and wonderful things his company has done for other contractors in the past, and they were prepared to do for him if a situation every arose.

The two weeks came and went, and as if on que, the follow-up meeting with the industry consultant was held.

Eager to hear what the consultant had to say, the contractor suspended any type of opening decorum and started pushing the consultant for information. Somewhat slow and hesitant to respond, the industry consultant started out with a couple empathetic comments. He then pulls out a piece of paper and hands it to the contractor. On the piece of paper was a list of prominent claims attorneys practicing in the State of California who the industry consultant suggested the contractor call for legal advice relating to the matter. Saying in so many unspoken words: "Sorry, we can't help you...good luck!"

Visibly distraught by what had just happened, the contractor sat quietly for a moment to collect his thoughts. Trying to make the awkward silence a bit more palatable, the industry consultant adds, "I'm sorry, we couldn't have done more" type of comment before the contractor abruptly ends the meeting.

Left with no real good options and almost two months down the road from when the conflict first started, it was quickly becoming desperation time for the contractor. So in one last ditch effort, the contractor decided to call one of the attorneys on the list provided to him by the industry consultant.

Unbeknownst to the contractor, though, the issue had been abruptly taken out of his hands by the owner/developer, because a few days later, after the meeting with the industry consultant, the owner/developer called to ask the contractor if he would join them at a meeting scheduled for the following Monday, three days before Thanksgiving.

Seeing this as an optimistic sign that the owner/developer had finally come to a more rational negotiating position in order to keep the project moving forward, the contractor euphorically sensed that some reasonable settlement would be reached at the meeting that would once and for all allow them to get past the financial and emotional stress being applied to the company. Stress that was affecting everyone, not just the owners of the company.

Monday came, and with high expectations of things turning out well for them, the contractor decided to bring along his wife, who was armed with all the outstanding payment records. Then, after some brief introductions and pleasantries, one of the owners of the development group heading up the renovation project, calmly drops a totally unexpected bomb on the conversation. He announced to the contracting couple that they were exercising the "Termination for Convenience" clause in the contract, and, that the contractor, with his one hundred or so employees still working on site, had seventy-two hours to vacate the property of all personnel, tools, and equipment; which meant, everything had to be off the project before Thanksgiving.

Time for a Mental Note

Contractors should never make the mistake to think that an owner will never exercise the "Termination for Convenience" clause found in just about every contract written in construction. I have been a part of a number of these types of events, on large scale projects no less, and it does happen. As part of the strategy going into a project, contractors must look at setting up their costs accounting means, methods, policies, and procedures from the standpoint that at any given time an owner can bring any portion of the project, i.e., scope of work, to an untimely halt.

Literally stunned and totally caught off guard that someone would actually kick their company off of a project, the contractor asked in response if there was any other option that could be worked out. In response, the owner/developer replied that too much time had already passed, and with no communications or movement on the issue from the contractor, other commitments had already been made.

Then, the contractor asked about payment. The owner/developer replied that payment discussions would happen at a later date once the full impact of the contractor being removed from the project was known. At that point, the meeting was over.

Arriving back at the main office, the contractor immediately reached out to the claims attorney he had been in contact with prior to the meeting. The attorney's advice in effect was to get everything off the property within seventy-two hours as the contract states because the owner/developer does have the right to seize it after the deadline.

So for the next two days, the contractor literally shut down all non-essentially aspects of the business and proceeded to make countless trips to and from the job site in an all-out effort to get everything off the property by the Wednesday deadline. Instead of paying electricians for what they were trained to do, the contractor was now paying them to demobilize company tools, equipment, and material from the site.

Wednesday arrived, and as the last truck full of the company's tools, equipment, and material left the site around mid-afternoon, it was now time to say good-bye to all the craftsmen that had been working on the project for almost a year. Knowing what was about to happen, most if not all, understood and quietly picked up their check for the last time and went to the union hall to sign "The Book."

In the end, the owner/developer continued to string along the contractor for months on end without making any substantial payments to relieve the company's financial and emotional stress. After about eight months of going back and forth with the owner/developer and incurring more and more attorney fees, the contractor had had enough and eventually agreed to settle for a substantially discounted amount that had been owed for so many months.

After a handful of years struggling to get back on their feet, the husband and wife contractor combo finally shut down the business down, sold their house, and retired to another state. What was once an extremely bright future for the couple and their employees, quickly went down the tubes in what seemed to be in the blink of an eye.

What lies ahead for businesses of all kinds in the US in terms of demographic shifts over the next fifty or so years will be unlike any seen over the past one hundred years, thanks mainly to unbridled immigration policies and an ever-widening communication gap between diverging generations exacerbated by advancements in technology. Fortunately, though, the impacts of these demographic shifts can be predictable with 70 to 80 percent accuracy, so as long as people are paying close attention to what's going on around them. Unfortunately, though at this time, most aren't.

I granted you that there will always be business failures caused by inexperienced and undercapitalized generational owners, but the economic impacts caused by (a) systemic labor shortages, (b) fragmented acceptance of technological changes, (c) a widening immigrant culture, (d) social media, (e) rising interest rates, (f) rising taxes, (g) restrictions on borrowing, (h) political unrest, and (i) language barriers will have such profound and devastating impacts to traditional business acumen that unsuspecting business owners, executives, and entrepreneurs will never see what hit them until it's too late.

For the past one hundred years, business owners, executives, and entrepreneurs have been taught that personal relationships were all that matter when it came to servicing the needs of customers and generating top line revenues. Relationships that had been fortified over time by exceptional performances and having a stellar reputation throughout the community.

In the business sectors of US economy today, business owners, executives, and entrepreneurs have to have the ability to step back and objectively take an honest look at what's really going on within the operational framework of their respective companies. Unfortunately, however, for most business owners, executives, and entrepreneurs operating today, they limit their objectivity to one of two outcomes related to their business: (a) how much profit is being generated, and/or (b) how much revenue growth is being secured in the future. Arguably, neither of which being true measurements of operational performance or how the community at-large perceives their reputation for being a value-added, quality company.

So why do business owners, executives, and entrepreneurs limit themselves to just these two parameters? It's mainly because they have been conditioned to think this way given the fact that these are the two parameters that matter most to analysts and investors on Wall Street. In other words, are companies making their numbers from one financial reporting period to the next?

Time for a Mental Note

"When companies...[are] living by so-called making the numbers, they do a lot of things that are really counter to the long-term interests of the business." (Warren Buffett)

From an operational perspective today, most businesses are plagued by a number of acute but systemic reasons that lead to the fundamental decay of their operational life cycle. There are also a number of terminal reasons as well that cause businesses in some industries to come and go at an alarming rate like construction. For example:

a) An inability to achieve and maintain the required level of operational alignment, synergy, and liquidity

b) An inability to maintain an acceptable reputation for doing business that leave customers with no other choice but to look for alternative service providers and value-added resellers

c) An inability to attract, train, and maintain highly qualified employees that bring added value to the organization

d) An inability to create and maintain healthy sales revenue

e) Maintaining antiquated policies and procedures that are insufficient to survive unforeseen financial and economic events that can cripple the company beyond the point of salvaging

f) An inability to keep employees and assets safe from harm

g) An inability to continuously improve on current levels of operational performance

h) An inability to effectively communicate with employees and customers

i) An inability to spot future trends in the marketplace or shifts in demographics

j) An inability to grasp the advancements in technology, innovation, automation, and artificial intelligence

k) An inability to create a culture of continuous process improvement

Not only do these systemic and terminal reasons exist today, but it's pretty evident that they will also be present in the future. A future that will also be compounded by additional systemic and terminal concerns such as the following:

a) Labor shortages, particularly in sectors of the US economy like construction, which will continue to draw international immigrants looking for a better life for themselves and their families. In doing so, this will eventually create overwhelming language barriers and cultural conflicts between employers, employees, and customers.

b) As the numerous problems being created by an ever-increasing immigrant workforce multiply, technological innovation, e.g., automation and artificial intelligence, will finally be allowed to supplement manual means and methods requiring contractors to find ways to integrate both manpower and machinery in the most cost effective manner possible.

c) As technology forces the design, manufacturing, distribution, and construction sectors of the US economy to become more integrated, interdependent, and seamless, all four business sectors will find themselves realigning with one another and physically combining their operations under one umbrella, and eventually competing against one another as opposed to being complimentary as strategic partners like most are today.

d) Because the federal government, as well as so many state and local governments, is so deep in debt, interest rates will begin to rise as a means to attract more investors, domestic and international, so that agencies will still be able to pay for government funded programs and services. This will also mean that it will become more difficult and more expensive for companies to borrow money to pay for short-term obligations and/or fuel future growth.

e) EDI (electronic exchange of business documents) will continue to replace paper-based data exchange operations as the race to the "cloud" continues by the major tech companies. Digital platforms, algorithms, data storage, viral marketing, and communications through social media will all become the new norm, and no longer the exception.

f) Global banking, or the exchange of commerce—i.e., financial transactions—will move toward a digital asset and payment system similar to what Bitcoin has been trying to launch since 2008. Eventually, most, if not all, commercial exchanges will transact directly between users without an intermediary such as a bank, credit union, insurance agent, government agency, investment group, etc.

g) Cost accounting and financial reporting will be recorded and available in real-time through the integration of buyer and seller data bases.

It is absolutely true that in the coming decades without the proper training, awareness, and experience, business owners, executives, and entrepreneurs attempting to be successful in any industry will constantly be repeating the failures of the past if they continue to only focusing on how much profit and revenue they can generate from one financial reporting period to the next, all the while ignoring demographic and technological shifts being embraced by their competitors and customers alike. Not to mention, ignoring the basic fundamentals of operational alignment, synergy, and liquidity.

Background: Kansas City, MO

In 1996, a well-established medium sized electrical contractor had just been purchased by a well-intending computer software salesman who knew little to nothing about operating a construction company? In order to make the purchase, the computer software salesman knew he was going to have to courageously risk most of his families' savings in order to satisfy the terms of the deal.

As a point of reference, prior to the purchase of the company, the current owners of the company had focused their attention for over twenty years on industrial and military type projects. Successful in their own right, and now well into their late fifties and early sixties, the owners had made a decision that they were ready for change in lifestyle, and viewed the sale of their company as an opportunity to transition out of the daily grind of contracting.

Anxious to make his mark on the local construction market, and knowing he needed to create a sustainable top line growth trend in order to meet payment obligations relating to his purchase agreement, the new owner set his sights on landing one of the largest commercial projects to come along in a while. It was a new federal courthouse being built in the downtown area.

Time for a Mental Note

To put this decision into perspective, you have to remember that the contractor had a twenty year history of successfully performing industrial and military type projects. Projects that the company's estimators, supervisors, and field installers were well trained and experienced to handle and deliver. And as a medium sized contractor, most, if not all, of the company's contracts were less than $2.5 million and required little to no bonding. The new owner has now made the decision that he wants to pursue an extremely large and complex commercial type project that the estimating staff, supervisors, and field installers had little to no experience with, and, the project would require a substantial bid bond, along with a subsequent payment and performance bond.

The day of the bid found two other electrical contractors in the area interested in pursuing the project as well. Unbeknownst to the new owner at the time, the highest of the three electrical bids came in at well over $11 million, while the second lowest bid came in at just over $10 million. The new owner's bid was just above $9 million—a 10 percent differential from the second lowest bid, which by industry standards would be considered at the highest end of a reasonable delta, but still in the acceptable range. Adding to the attractiveness of the new owner's low bid by all the general contractors taking the sub bids was the unit price component of the bid format that his estimating staff felt reasonably comfortable about in terms of the profit contained within each unit cost.

As word of the bidder's numbers started to leak out from the unsuccessful general contractors who had bid the job, eventually it was revealed where the new owner's bid fell in comparison to the other two bidders. Undaunted by the difference in his company's bid as compared to the second and third bidder, the new owner quickly moved to secure the award of the project with the low general contractor.

By this time in the ownership transition, which didn't include the new cost and revenue stream for the large courthouse project, the new owner appeared to be struggling a bit to make both installment payments to the previous owners and payments to venders who supplied the material and equipment to the ongoing operation. For weeks on end, cash flow from operations was continuing to put the business under a tremendous amount of stress. Then, cash flow reaches a critical state. The contractor had run so low on available cash to pay his current obligations that venders started putting trade payable accounts on "COD" (cash on delivery), which did nothing more than exacerbate the situation and put the operation under even more stress.

Admirably working day and night to keep the doors of his business open, the new owner was finally able to start seeing some substantial cash flow coming in from the progress payments of the new courthouse project. So much so, that he was not only able to bring trade payable accounts current again with venders, but he was actually able to start paying down some of the debt he had incurred from the bank in order to support the ongoing operations of the company.

Time for a Mental Note

During the early stages of most major projects, and assuming the schedule of values (SOV) presented each month as backup to progress payments is properly loaded with anticipated profit on front end items to be billed, cash flow trends tend to accelerate the gap between the actual cash being received from generating revenue billings and the actual costs being incurred, as was the case with the new courthouse project. Unfortunately, though, there will come a point during the progress cycle of the project where costs incurred during a thirty-day application period will far outpace those of the available revenue that can be billed for during the same period, consequently, creating a negative cash flow.

However, the cash flow reprieve didn't last long. As to be expected, the large courthouse project start absorbing more and more of the company's available resources in order to support the ongoing construction progress. So much so, that attention was now being taken away from replacing the exhausted revenue stream from other projects in the new owner's backlog; and as a consequence, further increasing the level of negative cash flow. It became painfully obvious at this point that the adverse effects of taking on the large courthouse project were starting to take its toll on the entire operation of the company.

Returning back to the bank once again for more working capital to operate the business, the new owner was told that he had reached the level of risk the bank was willing to undertake in loaning him anymore money. So the new owner aggressively launched a survival strategy, turning all of his employee's focus from their primary responsibilities of operating the business to billing whatever revenue was left in the backlog, and, aggressively collecting as much cash as possible in the shortest amount of time. Unfortunately in the end, those efforts were not going to be enough.

Six months or so later, the consequences of this strategy started coming to fruition when it was realized that while more resources and costs were being incurred at the new courthouse project, the amount of cash generated from the backlog of work being exhausted was no longer available. As a result, it wasn't long before the cycle of CODs related to trade payable accounts started showing up again from the vender community.

After a series of seemingly desperate "Hail Mary" maneuvers to keep the doors open, the new owner knew the end was near. He also knew by this time that he had limited options going forward to meeting the required level of operational alignment, synergy, and liquidity.

By any stretch of the imagination, devastating stories like this one are not uncommon in a number of industries. In fact, they are repeated time and again throughout multiple industries thanks in part to the lack of training, awareness, and experience of new business owners, executives, and entrepreneurs that unwittingly get themselves into trouble as they climb over their industry's extremely low barriers to entry.

That said, not all the blame can be laid at the feet of inexperienced new business owners, executives, and entrepreneurs that get their businesses into trouble from time to time. The finger of blame can also be pointed directly at others charged with supporting and guiding the business as well. Equity partners, internal managers and supervisors, legal counsel, accountants and auditors, lenders, insurance and bonding agents, all have played a role to some degree in helping companies find their way to the steps of liquidation.

Background: Clearwater, FL

Through a series of ownership transactions stemming all the way back to the mid-1970s, a large regional specialty contractor, who had built itself into a highly respected organization over the previous twenty years, found itself at a cross-roads. It was now the middle of the 1990s and the current ownership group had decided that it was time to sell the company outright to whomever could present the best deal. But there was a problem, not everyone thought it was such a great idea to sell the company; especially the senior members of the operating group who had little to no ownership stake in the company.

The decision to sell the company by the ownership group also came at a time when the "roll-up" of specialty contractors' era was in full swing; and with all the excitement being generated from Wall Street, along with other sectors of the economy related to the construction industry, it didn't take long for the ownership group to start prospecting for a would-be buyer.

Then one day, a call came into the operating president of the large specialty contractor from the ownership group informing him that the they had found a consolidator who would be willing to enter into a deal. The first step in the agreed upon process was for the consolidator and operating president to meet face-to-face in order to exchange pleasantries and discuss what each other was prepared to bring to the table. After the meeting, there was no question the consolidator wanted to continue moving forward with the buy-out, however, the operating president wasn't having any of it and neither was the other senior operating managers once the president got back and reported to them what he had heard from the consolidator.

It was now roughly 1998, and it appeared the enthusiasm of Wall Street investors clamoring over the prospect of investing in the concept of contractor "roll ups" was almost at a fever's pitch. So much so, that even equity managers of high income clients were also looking into getting in the game as well, not from a consolidator's perspective, but in terms of being an equity partner for platform companies looking to expand. For whatever reason, Wall Street saw potential in owning specialty contractors.

Toward the end of 1998, to the satisfaction of the senior operating members, the large specialty contractor was eventually sold to an equity investment group looking to balance out their risk portfolio. And although the purchase of the large specialty contractor was well below the level of investment they preferred, the equity investment group went forward with the transaction in the hope that, sooner rather than later, the large specialty contractor would undertake an aggressive expansion program and reach a size they were normally used to investing in at the time.

As the late 1990s gave way to the new millennium, and at the insistence of the new board of directors led by the equity investment group, the large regional contractor did expand by this time from a handful of branch locations throughout the state of Florida to eleven office locations throughout the southeast. It seemed as though all the stars were lining up for the equity investment group searching for a higher level of revenue and profitability.

With a reasonable amount of debt on the books to support both ongoing operations and the expansion effort, there came a time that the senior management of the specialty contractor started warning the board of directors that any further expansion would more than likely require the need for a further infusion of cash. Although the large specialty contractor had performed very well during its initial expansion phase, resources and core competencies had now been stretched to the point where any further expansion would require additional support from the equity investment group.

As 2002 rolled around, the large specialty contractor had revenues in excess of $110 million, almost double the amount from when they were initially purchased by the equity investment group. Confident in the operational group, the board of directors voted for further expansion in the coming year. This time, the expansion program would not necessarily focus on adding additional branch locations, but rather an expansion of complementary service offerings and deliverables. Complementary service offerings and deliverables that up until this time had either been systematically avoided in the past, or, subcontracted out to other smaller contracting firms. It was an excellent strategy on paper; and one in which the equity investment group was willing to provide the additional funding to make it happen.

As one of eleven branch managers assembled for the big announcement passed down from the board of directors, I can assure you the new expansion program was met with mixed emotions. I wouldn't say we were bewildered at the announcement because we all had a lot of faith in the senior management team that was guiding the company, but we were all now being asked to look beyond our comfort zones and embrace another expansion program with limited amounts of detail on how it was actually supposed to be implemented.

Over the course of the next year, it was as if the company was reacting to a massive infusion of steroids steered toward nothing but revenue growth across eleven additional P & L statements. Watching all this unfold and scratching our heads in somewhat disbelief, the branch managers continued to march on as if we could once again weather another expansionary storm that was brewing.

But it didn't take long before complaints from branch managers starting to surface more frequently about resources being stretch to capacity and their need to hire and/or train more qualified personnel across the entire support spectrum. Then, as if on que, those complaints about the lack of resource support got compounded by complaints from both the vender and subcontractor communities not getting paid in a timely manner—furthering the need for additional funding by the equity investment group.

As time continued to march on, and by this time, all the branch managers had assumed that the negative cash flow trend plaguing the company was primarily due to the expansion effort, but as it turned out, that was only one part of what was truly going on with the cash flow of the company. Thanks to two of the larger branches, it was announced that their efforts to collect over $3 million in added costs and profit were failing, and failing miserably.

Still holding our own without an infusion from the equity investment group, and still picking up large amounts of future revenue, it was now early 2004 and the company had reached its tipping point from all the operational alignment, synergy, and liquidity problems plaguing the company. There was no question that the company was in dire straits from a "liquidity" standpoint between all the upfront costs being incurred from the latest expansion effort and the two major projects under contract that had massive amounts of unresolved change orders sapping the cash flow.

Working feverishly day and night, all the executives and branch managers were doing everything they could to enhance the company's cash flow. Then one day, the call finally came that the equity investment group was going to provide a significant amount of funding to relieve the debilitating strain on the company's cash flow. Why the funding took so long, no one would say exactly, but it really didn't matter at that point. All that mattered was the large specialty contractor was once again on reasonably solid financial footing, and returning what appeared to be an acceptable level of profit back to the equity investment group.

As the fourth quarter of 2004 approached, and having just weathered an extremely debilitating cash flow problem, the large specialty contractor seemed to now have the wind at its back and looking forward to closing out the year and preparing to make the New Year a more productive one with a lot less stress. With healthy revenues continuing to flow into the company, everything seemed to be falling back in line for the company—2005 was scheduled to be a banner year as revenues were projected to surpass the $135 million mark.

Then, one day and out of the blue, the CEO of the company received a call from the equity investment group requesting a meeting in New York; which wasn't an abnormal request since the CEO was used to making regular trips to board meetings at the equity investment group's office. However, this request was different. This time, the CEO was asked to bring along with him a representative of the surety company who wrote the bid, payment, and performance bonds for the majority of the company's projects. Puzzled by the request, the CEO went ahead and scheduled the trip.

Time for a Mental Note

Mentioning the surety company is extremely important here because over 95 percent of all the large specialty contractor's work had a bid, and/or payment and performance bond guarantying that 100 percent of material and labor cost obligations would be met. So long as the surety company had confidence in the large specialty contractor's ability to consistently generate a certain level of profit, and, finish the required scope of work and pay for all outstanding costs incurred by the projects, the surety company would continue to provide the required bonding to the large specialty contractor; which would also allow the large specialty contractor to continue to pursue more work, i.e., revenue growth.

As the CEO and representative of the surety company walked into the meeting room, the CEO happened to notice a number of folks that he had never seen before. Once the meeting was convened, it didn't take long for the CEO to find out exactly why he was requested to be in New York, and who the new faces were that joined the meeting.

The equity investment group had decided to pull all of their equity out of the company effective immediately, and the new faces in the meeting were the attorneys who supported the decision. Their rationale for coming to such a decision, "the deal" was just not large enough for them to support any longer, and that it was time to pull the money out and invest it elsewhere.

Confused, shocked, and somewhat bewildered, the CEO sat motionless for a few seconds in order to collect his thoughts before responding. He then very calmly informed the entire group assembled at the meeting that if they truly intend to move forward with their divestiture in the company, especially in an expedited and non-orderly liquidation manner, that they have to in effect, shut down the company and subsequently lose all of their investment. And as if on que, one of the investment bankers spoke up and said that their course of action was at the advice of their legal counsel, and it was not conceivable to think they would lose any money from their exit strategy given the current state of the company's solvency.

After the meeting had concluded, the CEO paid a one-on-one visit to the investment banker who actually put the deal together about six years prior. The CEO proceeded to educate the banker on the fact that any contract work with payment and performance bond coverage was under the fiduciary control of the bonding company, i.e., Surety Company, not the equity group; and the receivables relating to those projects could not be touched by the equity group. As a consequence of the fact that over 95 percent of the company's work was bonded, the surety company controlled most of the cash on hand, along with any receivables being collected to cover the costs of the actual work under contract.

Time for a Mental Note

Bonded receivables are to be held in a separate account and are only to be used in relation to the work that is covered under the surety company bond. All too often, though, by the very nature of contracting, both bonded and non-bonded receivables become comingled in support of the ongoing operations of the company—a reasonably acceptable process so long as proper accounting practices are adhered to and easily discernable in case of an audit. However, tapping into bonded receivables can quickly become a huge problem for a contractor if he or she is no longer able to cash flow both bonded and non-bonded operations.

Still not willing to reconsider their decision, the investment banker reiterated that their attorneys have looked into the matter and have advised them otherwise. Left with no other options, the CEO returned to his office the very next morning.

Waiting for him at his office was a letter from the surety company stating in effect that they were no longer going to provide any further bonding support for the company, and that they were in effect taking control of all related receivables generated from work that currently had a payment and performance bond insuring the project. Although foretold by the CEO just a day earlier, it was not what the equity investment group, nor their legal counsel, had been prepared for.

Three months or so later, and unable to secure any future work due to the lack of bonding and financial support, the once vibrant and solvent specialty contracting company filed for bankruptcy protection.

Here you had an established company with proven operational leadership, moderately healthy revenues continuing to come in the door, making a profit, and a market economy that was poised to support growth and prosperity. But with one uninformed decision by a senior equity partner, the operational alignment, synergy, and liquidity of the company quickly reached an unsustainable level and the business was ultimately forced to liquidate all of its holdings and assets.

I can't say it enough times throughout this book, business owners, executives, and entrepreneurs who allow themselves to be guided solely by hitting short-term levels of profit and revenue projections while ignoring the internal performance levels of their operation are making a huge mistake when it comes to meeting both their short-term and long-term obligations. Business owners, executives, and entrepreneurs have got to hold true to their internal convictions when everyone around them starts to get skittish about missing their marks when the least bit of bad or discouraging news gets announced.

Background: Merriam, KS

Remember the well-intending computer software salesman I just told you about who knew little to nothing about operating a construction company but made the decision anyway to purchase a well-established medium sized electrical contractor. This is the rest of the story.

After a series of misguided decisions spanning about eighteen months, the new owner found himself strapped for cash and desperately trying to avoid liquidation.

Putting the word out on the street through secondary channels, i.e., banks, accounting firms, and law firms, the new owner was in search of an investor or competitor to partner up with. As luck would have it, most of the feedback pointed to another medium-sized contractor in the area who had been in business going on three generations, and who at times had been experiencing their own financial struggles.

After a couple of meetings between the owners of the two contracting companies, confidentiality agreements were exchanged as well as three years of financial statements. By all indications, at least the two owners felt there was some viability in bringing the two companies together.

Then, it was the owner's respective attorneys and accountants turn to weigh in. Each quickly building legal and financial barriers around their respective clients in an all-out attempt not to lose any future business. Instinctively, one group of advisors knew they would no longer be needed once the merger went through, so it was in their best interest to throw up as many roadblocks as possible during this preliminary time. But in the end, with each of the owners knowing they needed the other for the deal to go through in order not to let over seventy years of combined contracting experience go down the tubes, the owners pushed on.

As the owners finally found their way past all the wrangling between their advisors, it was now time to face their biggest challenge, convincing one of their respective banks to accept the large amount of consolidated debt being brought to the table. Unbeknownst at the time to each of the contractor's owners, each bank was looking for their own exit strategy in order to get out from under their own respective liabilities, but after reviewing each contractor's balance sheet, it became painfully obvious to each banker which bank was going to be left holding the bigger bag if the deal didn't go through and the contractors ultimately closed their doors for good.

So the "risk versus reward" decision by the one banker who was holding the most debt came down to (a) Do I call the contractor's notes and force him into an involuntary liquidation with the hope of mitigating the bank's current exposure? or (b) Do I fund the payoff of the other contractor's debt and increase my risk by another 50 percent in the hopes that the economies of scale generated by the merged companies would accelerate additional profits being made as a means to paying down the additional risk sooner rather than later? In the end, the banker gambled and agreed to fund the merger of the two struggling contractors.

Post-merger, all seemed to be going well for the first year or so, mainly due to the company having an additional person focused solely on billings and collecting monies owed to the company. Although cash flow would get a little tight at times, overall, the company's level of operational alignment, synergy, and liquidity continued to trend in a positive direction.

Also too, everyone from the contractor's ownership group to senior managers in the accounting department seemed to be diligent in their watching all the accounts at the bank in order to insure none of them would be overdrawn; especially during the time each month when the benefit payment to the Local union came due on a particular day. Confidence in the newly merged company by the bank was definitely on the rise as receivables continued to be on an upward trajectory each month.

Then one day, the contractor decided to pursue, and was subsequently awarded, a reasonably large, labor-intensive, fast–track project with one of the local utility companies. Knowing that cash flow was already tight, along with the fact that the customer made it perfectly clear that there was not going to be any relief to the proposed construction schedule, one of the owners of the company called the bank and explained the situation. Although the bank was hesitant to increase the contractor's current line of credit, the owner insisted that it would only be a temporary situation given the short duration of the project.

Ultimately, the owner provide enough convincing evidence that the bank agreed to temporarily extend the contractor's line of credit under the condition that a "floor," i.e., minimum amount of available funds, would be set on the main depository account, and if the floor became breached for any reason, the bank would set off all accounts and discussions of a forced liquidation would immediately ensue. It was a risk the contractors were willing to take.

Concerned with the condition of a "floor" being in place, in conjunction with the procurement process of the fast track project, the contractors were feeling reasonably confident that level of operational alignment, synergy, and liquidity would be sustainable in the coming weeks so long as they could stay ahead of fast-track project's billing process. Unfortunately, six weeks into the project, the company's level of operational alignment, synergy, and liquidity started to trend in the negative direction as other projects in the company's pipeline started to gear up as well with their own manpower and material procurement needs.

Time for a Mental Note

Unlike trade payables where payments can be extended to 90 days in some cases, most rank and file employees need to be paid weekly; which means, a company's payroll account is the first to be funded each week.

As a union contractor, and knowing that on the fifteenth of every month the local union had to have a check in hand for the benefits being paid to bargaining unit employees, the contractor's accounting department was responsible each month to project how much the benefits payment to the local union was scheduled to be. As the company's level of operational alignment, synergy, and liquidity continued to decline, a mild panic started to set in with the owners who knew breaching the "floor" imposed by the bank would ultimately be the end of the company.

As word started to leak out that the contractor might be facing more financial difficulties, concerns amongst the vender/subcontractor community also started rising again as well with increased calls coming in about when they could come by the office and pick up their monthly payables check—a process in lieu of the customary waiting for the checks to be mailed out and eventually received. Not wanting to alarm the vender/subcontractor community any more than they were already, the contractor agreed to alter the payment policy process and allowed folks to come by the office on certain days of the month to pick up their payable checks. Here again, this did nothing more than put additional stress on an already stretched to the max cash flow situation.

Eventually, word made its way to the Local union that the contractor might be having financial troubles and they should be on the lookout for union member checks starting to bounce. The Local union was also now on high alert with regards to the benefit payment that was due by the fifteenth of the month. It was as if everyone at the company, and the construction community at large, was on contractor-watch, waiting for it to eventually fail financially.

As each subsequent month came and went with no incident of a bounce check or missed benefit payment, things didn't seem to get any better as one key manager of the company after another started to quit the company in pursuit of a more stable environment. Once word got out that key managers were leaving the company, field employees as well started to follow suit. But month after month, nothing changed for the contractor's senior managers and accounting staff who continued to meet daily in order to keep an eye on the company's cash flow needs.

Time for a Mental Note

As a signatory (union) contractor, most of the field employees belong to a local union where external and internal work/membership rules apply. One of the internal membership rules that a number of Local unions employ is that all out-of-work members must sign a referral book that provides for a fair call-out process when manpower needs are requested by contractors. Members also have the right to refuse a referral without losing their position on the book. If word happens to get out that a certain contractor is having a difficult time meeting payroll, perceived or otherwise, it is very difficult for that contractor to get anyone to take the referral—leaving the contractor in a very precarious situation with his or her customer.

It was now October 1997, just over a year into the merger, and although the merger had seen some ups and downs the company was still on relatively stable footing. Then came that time of the month again, the fifteenth, when the benefit payment came due to the Local union. It was a Wednesday, and like the transaction had been processed the many months prior, the check was written and delivered to the Local union well in advance of the published deadline.

The next day, Thursday, and for some unknown reason, representatives of the Local union took it upon themselves to call the bank to inquire if the check had cleared for funding. When the representatives heard that it hadn't, the Local went into a mild panic thinking the worst was about to happen. Then calls between the Local union and contractor were exchanged and reassurances given that all was normal and there was nothing to be concerned about.

Then, Friday comes, roughly two days after the sizable check had been deposited in the Local union's bank account. Again, calls from the local union were made to the bank and they were once again told that the check had not yet cleared. Unbeknownst to the contractor that the local union had been engaged in these ongoing exchanges with the bank, the owners and senior managers went about their daily activities as if it was business as usual.

By about noon, word had started to spread that the contractor had bounced their benefits check, even though there was no truth to what was being rumored. By 2:00 PM, most of the three-hundred-plus field employees had abandoned their respective job sites and went to the local union hall to find out what was going on. By 3:00 PM, most of the field supervisors still on their respective job sites started to call the office inquiring as to what might be going on.

After hearing word that most of the field employees had abandoned their jobs before quitting time, the owners of the contracting company contacted the Local union around 3:30 PM to see what was going on, and why the employees left their jobs. The local union responded that most of the employees would not be back to work on the following Monday because the benefit's check had bounced and they were afraid their members' paychecks were next.

Trying to convince the local union there was mistake and that the check just needed time to clear, the Local union responded to the owners by saying that they had tried repeatedly to get the check to clear for two days and it was the bank who told them that the check was being delayed from clearing (as opposed to it just hadn't cleared yet). The owners asked the local union to sit tight while they contacted the bank to see what was actually going on.

In utter disbelief with how the entire scenario was playing out the way it was, the owners of the contracting company immediately called the bank to find out what was going on on their end. The banker said that he had no idea other than the fact that someone from the Local union had been calling, asking if a particular checked had been cleared yet, and it hadn't. The contractor then informed the banker of the conversation that just took place with the Local union, and that in effect, operations were in limbo with the Local union until the check cleared. The banker then asked for the owners to give him a few minutes and he would call them back.

After about thirty minutes had passed, one of the senior VPs of the bank called the majority owner of the company to inform him that a decision had been made to set off all of the contractor's accounts, and that the owners needed to be in their office first thing Monday morning to discuss an "orderly" liquidation of the company's assets. Bewildered by such a drastic measure undertaken by the bank, the majority owner asked if the bank had really thought this decision through. The VP replied that they had, and that this was the appropriate time for them to limit their liability supporting the company.

Immediately following the conversation with the bank's VP, the owners of the contracting company starting discussions with a number of legal advisors. Working throughout the weekend it became painfully obvious to the owners that the company was no longer going to be able to operate come Monday morning, and the dire situation needed to be made abundantly clear to the bank's executives and legal counsel as soon as possible.

As the meeting on Monday got underway, it was obvious the bank, along with their legal counsel, had no idea what chain of events were launch the previous Friday by the uninformed actions they decided to undertake. They came to the meeting with their in-house legal counsel thinking the discussion was going to be more about how the owners would help the bank dissolve the assets and collect all the receivables. Unfortunately for the bank, they were unaware of the fact that over 50 percent of the current receivables were actually related to bonded work and did not belong to them. In order to collect those receivables they were going to need cooperation from the surety company.

Needless to say, the once pompous and arrogant bankers, thinking they had just saved their institution millions of dollars, quickly coward in disbelief to an attitude of "What did we just do?"

Everyone realizes and understands that equity investment groups, lenders, and surety companies need to make a profit, as well as protect their own downside risk, but in doing so, they have got to keep the best interest of the collective group in mind when it comes to making tough decisions that could ultimately lead to a disastrous outcome. Time and again, I have seen and heard where an investment group, lender, or surety company got anxious for some uninformed reason about their investment, or a level of risk concerning their involvement with a particular business, and immediately acted in their own self-interest as a means to protecting any down side loss or risk regardless of the outcome to the collective group. In doing so, they unintentionally seal the fate of the business they were supposedly supporting.

The concern I have going into the next century with the way increasing amounts of debt is being incurred by the federal, state, and local government is that lending additional funds to the community at-large is going to get tighter and more expensive as time goes on. So much so, that it will start impacting local communities in a number of ways:

- With the availability to funds getting tighter and more expensive it is very likely that construction growth in certain states, who are experiencing population decreases, will see sharp declines in construction activities. Public tax dollars and private monies will start being diverted toward the renovation and repair of existing facilities in lieu of new construction.

- In areas of the country that are experiencing population growth, construction spending will increase as well. The rate at which construction spending will take place will be directly proportionate to the tax revenues being generated and the rate at which interest will be added to borrowed funds. This will also precipitate the need for more accurate and real-time accounting methods and procedures, along with an increased involvement by the financial community in construction activities.

- Beginning around 2030, if not before, construction contracting in the Midwest and Northeast will move more toward renovation and repair type design and installation, while the South and West will see design and construction activities increase in new, expansion, renovation, and repair type work.

- Billion-dollar, mega-construction projects will become more commonplace. If smaller contractors currently providing construction services are not looking to be swallowed up by larger more sophisticated contractors actively pursuing these types of mega-projects, smaller contractors will be forced to somehow have both the physical and financial resources made available to them in order to compete.

- Bonding of construction projects will become more prevalent and more expensive as projects continue to grow in size and complexity, and as more and more contractors default on contracts.

- Health insurance premiums, including workman's comp, are going to continue to rise and productivity on job sites are going to fall as the population ages and marijuana becomes legalized throughout the country—causing an increase in job-related accidents.

- Given the current labor shortages, and the influx of non-English speaking workers, contractors are absolutely going to be required to spend more money on training, employee retention, pre-fabrication, modularization of assemble materials, innovation, and automation if they plan to compete in the coming decades. The monies that will need to be spent will either have to be borrowed and/ or come out of cash flow, increasing the financial stress of the company.

It also needs to be said that the inherent risks found in a number of industries like construction are just not limited to the involvement of external third parties like the financial services sector. Internal risks are also present every day where the potential for a wrong decision by an employee, while on the job or before starting a workday, can actually lead to a fatal outcome. It is because of this ever-present danger and potential for physical harm to employees that the US Congress, in 1970, established the Occupational Safety and Health Administration (OSHA).

Background: St. Joseph, MO

In October 2005, an explosion ripped through a pork processing plant under construction in a small Midwestern town, killing one person and injuring at least fourteen others just days before production was to begin. Some of the victims were blown out of the plant by the blast, which collapsed part of the second floor and opened a gaping hole in the roof. Two other victims had to be freed from the rubble, including one pinned beneath a concrete wall.

The cause of the explosion occurred when a worker lit an acetylene torch after a gas valve had been left uncapped, allowing unscented gas to escape into some of the confined spaces within the facility. By all accounts, it was an accident with deadly consequences.

Initially, all signs pointed to one particular specialty contractor being responsible for the accident. A family-owned and operated specialty contractor with an excellent reputation throughout the community, and company that had been in business for roughly eighty years.

As is often the case when incidents and accidents like this occur in construction, insurance companies are immediately notified of the occurrence. Quickly responding to the notification, the contractor's insurance company immediately became engage with the process.

For the next two and a half years, it was nothing short of an agonizing time for all involved with the accident. Then, at some point, it was announced that the largest personal injury settlement in the history of Buchanan County, Missouri, had been reached by the attorneys representing twenty workers injured in the explosion. The family-owned contractor, along with three other defendants, which included the local gas company, agreed to pay $12.25 million.

The frightening part about this story, besides all the lives that had been disrupted by the accident, was the fact that had the other three defendants not been brought into the settlement, the family-owned company who had been in business for eighty years would have more than likely closed their doors, and leaving any family member who still retained an ownership position with the responsibility of paying any monetary differences out of pocket.

In order to be successful business owner over the past one hundred years or so, owners had to be willing to take some level of risk. Risks that were calculable and pretty much known or reasonably anticipated prior to any final decision being made. However, going forward into the future, not all risks are going to be as calculable, known, or reasonably assumed. In fact, as generations of new owners, managers, supervisors, and employees start to cross paths with one another as the demographics of the country continue to shift (racially, ethnically, politically, and financially) new risks will begin to manifest themselves at the peril of many unsuspecting business owners.

Time for a Mental Note

"The time to be pessimistic in your life is when the cost of failure is too high, making optimism the wrong attitude to have." (Mark Towers)

There is no question that owning a business, particularly one in the construction industry, is a very risky endeavor for any new or existing owner, executives, or entrepreneurs. It is a "business purpose" that comes with an inherent danger of loss to personal wealth, and at times, physical harm to employees. It is also why business owners must take the time to be diligent with every aspect of their operation and rely heavily on competent, trustworthy executives, managers, and supervisors who are also constantly being reminded of all the risks related to a specific business purpose.

I can assure you, and as history has shown, industries like construction do not provide for the luxury of business owners, executives, managers, or supervisors to engage in the practice of absentee management. Nor, do many industries provide a safe haven for business owners, executives, and entrepreneurs willing to turn a blind eye to demographic shifts, operational performance levels, and the future needs of customer; although many business owners, executives, and entrepreneurs actually do arrogantly walk that very thin line each and every day.

Operating at Peak Performance: Ignore It at Your Own Peril

As demographics continue to shift in the US and abroad, so too will the hue of cultures, beliefs, behavior, attitudes, value systems. Social norms that were once looked upon as important to previous generations are practically guaranteed not to be embraced the same way as future generations continue to mature.

In the US, we are already seeing changes to social norms playing out as the tech savvy generations, i.e., X and Y, are becoming more ethnically and racially tolerant than generations of the past. But unlike the generations of the past who came to work each day with a solid value system that embraced hard work, loyalty, and commitment, business owners today don't see the more recent generations that way.

What they do see are younger generations that are ill-prepared, somewhat lazy, preoccupied legends of young tattooed and body pierced candidates unable to meet the future demands of customers outside their own value based communities. In particular, the construction industry that is quickly becoming a multi-cultural environment spanning the entire spectrum of recent social norms.

Think about the seriousness of what I just raised here for a second. Industries like construction have known for almost thirty years now that it will be facing a devastating labor shortage as the twenty-first-century unfolded. But yet, complacency, lack of leadership, and an inability to effectively address the problem, has now manifested the original problem into an even bigger, more complicated one with language barriers, immigration enforcement, safety concerns, and younger generations ignoring the value of being able to work with their hands instead of just with their fingers and mind.

Whether older generations like it or not, younger generations like Generations X and Y live in a much different world these days. It is a world that's all about technology, convenience, and a race to the top of organizational charts at the earliest possible age whether they're ready for the responsibility or not. They are two generations clothed in a cultural attitude of: "If technology can't fix the problem then it can't be fixed so why waste your time trying?" It's just a fact, manual labor is not a concept younger generations find appealing or want any part of. If you don't believe me, look around your neighborhood and count how many teenagers are helping out doing yardwork for their parents and grandparents like they did generations ago.

But there is hope. Younger generations like Generations X and Y have a distinct advantage over their parents and grandparents when it comes to recognizing the benefits of putting technology to use. Generations like X and Y, and soon to be on the scenes, Z, understand better than most that technology can solve a lot of problems that manual labor and human brain patterns simply can't.

Time for a Mental Note

"We cannot solve our problems with the same level of thinking that created them." (Albert Einstein)

By definition, and grammatically speaking, the term "high performance" is considered to be an adjective that describes an attitude that is attached to something measurable, such as *exceptional* quality, or *superior* service. But when most people think of "high performance" not all industries of the US economy like construction

113

is the first thing that usually pops into their minds. In fact, the first thing that usually comes to most people's mind when they hear the term "high performance" is automobiles, where the measurement of power, speed, maneuverability, reliability, and durability are constantly being monitored and evaluated in order to achieve the highest standards of performance.

In business, "*high performance*" companies like Amazon, Apple, and Microsoft for example are constantly measuring, monitoring, and evaluating every aspect of their operation in order to achieve the highest standards of performance required by their customers.

Performance standards like:

a) Operational Alignment, Synergy, and Liquidity
b) Digital Competency and Capability
c) Sociotechnical Systems (STS) Adoption and Compliance
d) Reputation
e) Innovation and Customer Development
f) Marketing and Community Involvement
g) Revenue Health and Growth
h) Cash Conversion Cycle
i) Employee Relations
j) Quality, Rework, and Defects
k) Continuous Process Improvement
l) Purchasing and Procurement
m) Total Preventative Maintenance
n) Scheduling and Project Controls
o) Safety

To meet the criteria of a "*high performance*" company, one could never be content with mediocrity, complacency, the status quo, or being operationally governed by perceived short-term successes of the past that could easily mask inefficiencies that automatically plague levels of performance in the future. Nor, could anyone ever ignore the future impacts created by shifting demographics, or the impacts that technology has on an industry as it continually builds upon previous generations of innovation, advancement, and expansion.

Time of a Mental Note

In 1964, the Xerox Corporation introduced to the consumer market what was at the time considered to be the first commercialized version of a modern day fax machine. Then in 1973, Xerox Corporation launched their own version of a minicomputer with its mouse, graphical user interface, expanded memory storage, bitmapped high resolution screen, and integrated software; which in effect, started the beginning of the end for their once revolutionary fax machine introduced just a decade prior. By the mid-1990s, companies like Apple, Dell, Gateway, along with a handful of others, had taken person computers to an entirely different level, effectively making fax machines obsolete.

Businesses today, and in the very near future, are going to be faced with the reality of having to modify their business models in order to achieve a certain level of performance. Not only will they be required to adopt the advantages of technology, but they will also be required to adopt managerial tools that include established metrics of behavior and business acumen that are emblematic of "*high performance*" companies such as the following: (a) a culture of operational alignment and continuous process improvement that culminates into positive cash flow; (b) an attitude toward meeting the future demands of customers; (c) an attitude toward risk management, loss prevention, and safety; (d) an attitude toward enhancing the communications and interpersonal relationships between management, employees, and customers; (e) a culture of total preventive maintenance of the entire organization; and (f) a continuous pursuit of digital acceptance and compliance, innovation, and automation.

So here's the $64,000 question: If being a "*high performance*" company is now, or will soon be, the operational standard by which all companies in the US should be striving to achieve each and every day, then why are so many businesses today, and are projected to be in the future, in trouble? In the construction industry alone it is estimated that three out of four contractors go out of business within 18 months of opening their doors, which is actually a lower percentage of failures than the overall average of all businesses throughout the US economy.

To answer this question we have to realize that most businesses in general who have endured a business failure will most likely tell you that their failure(s) could be traced to one or more of the following reasons:

- Under capitalization
- Poor market conditions
- Hiring the wrong people

So you have to ask yourself this question: If business failures can be boiled down to a specific number of known or anticipated problems, why can't business owners and their expert consultants immediately get out in front of the potential problems and solve them before disaster strikes, stemming the constant flow of business failures each and every year?

One reason is because some businesses are too far gone before industry consultants get called in by business owners to fix their problems, making it virtually impossible for them to right the ship in a timely manner. A second reason stems from the fact that business owners who actually do recognize potential problems ahead of time and endeavor to take preventative steps make the fatal mistake of letting costs drive their decision. Most business owners who fail do so by opting to bring in a less expensive consultant or consulting firm that in the end had absolutely no idea how to actually recognize and/or fix their problem.

Achieving and maintaining a required level of operational alignment, synergy, and liquidity through "high-performance" operations is a mandate for success as subsequent generations of owners and executives march into the future. And although a large number of business owners operating today will superciliously tell you that their own businesses perform at a very high level, I'm here to tell you that in my thirty-plus years in the construction industry many of these same business owners, if not all, have no earthly idea at what level of performance their operations are actually operating at from one day to the next. Nor, can they tell you with any degree of certainty if their current level of operational alignment, synergy, and liquidity will adequately support their current and future obligations.

If you find this hard to believe, the next time you happen to run into a self-proclaimed highly successful business owner ask him or her to show you what performance metrics they regularly use to measure, monitor, and evaluate their operational performance. Most will likely respond by either showing or telling you (a) how much profit they made in recent years or (b) how much revenue growth they've produced over the years. Both of which being the results, "after effects" if you will, of other operations functions and having absolutely nothing meaningful to do with measuring, monitoring, and evaluating their company's ongoing operational performance. In other words, although profits and revenues, in the eyes of current business owners, are commonly referred to as important metrics for businesses to measure, they are actually nothing more than the ever-changing by-products of vital operational functions that a business must effectively execute on a regular basis.

Throughout the history of the US, you will find one story after another about a business owner who had closed their doors for one reason or another but could actually tout the fact that their profit and revenue growth were performing at acceptable levels when the business was actually shut down. How could this be you ask?

It's a simple fact that businesses don't involuntarily go out of business because they can't generate a profit or create revenue growth. Businesses fail because they are unable to achieve and maintain the required level of operational alignment, synergy, and liquidity in order to meet current and future obligations. They become illiquid and unable to pay their employee's wages and bills.

Time for a Mental Note

If you look at the construction industry today, which again can be construed as a microcosm of the entire US economy, there are literally thousands of business owners in operation who have never been told about the importance of knowing the difference between operational by-products, i.e., profits and revenue growth, and the operational functions that constantly need to be measured, monitored, and evaluated in terms of their actual real-time performance. This lack of awareness and understanding is a fundamental flaw that plagues the entire construction industry, not to mention all the other business owners trying to operate companies throughout the US economy, and goes virtually unrecognized from one year to the next by most business owners.

History has proven time and again that no business owner—I REPEAT, no business owner, is immune from the pitfalls of their respective industries. Industries that at times seem truly unforgiving for business owners, executives, and entrepreneurs who arrogantly or accidentally:

a) Overlook the importance of achieving and maintaining the required level of operational alignment, synergy, and liquidity in order to meet current and future obligations of the company.

b) Brush aside obvious risk factors when pursuing familiar and unfamiliar types of contracts, especially in unfamiliar jurisdictions or areas of the country, not to mention the world.

c) Ignore the importance of continuous process improvement programs.

d) Ignore industry standards for safety, particularly if someone gets seriously injured or killed while on the job.

e) Choose the wrong business model, partner, or expansion program to pursue.

f) Ignore the fact that skilled labor shortages exist when pursuing contracts in certain areas of the country or world, and/or during expansionary times in a given market.

g) Embrace antiquated policies and procedures for operating a business that have been passed down from previous generations to the next.

h) Choose not to embrace technological advancements.

i) Choose the wrong customer.

j) Choose the wrong manager or supervisor to oversee an operation or business group.

k) Choose the wrong exit strategy or succession plan.

l) Spend enormous amounts of time away from operational duties and responsibilities in order to pursue outside interests.

m) Take the advice of a third party consultant, advisor, attorney, or accountant who may only have their own best interests in mind on an important decision going forward.

n) Ignore the effects of demographic shifts in the population.

Time for a Mental Note

"It is said that a fool learns from his own mistakes, a wise man from the mistakes of others."
(Otto von Bismarck)

Some may remember the economic crisis of 2007 through 2009 when the US and world economies found themselves in dire financial straits. Speculations as to the reasons why the crisis occurred in the first place have been well documented, but during this time there was a term heard over and over again, "Too big to fail," to the point it became seared into the minds of many even to this day. A theory if you will that embodied the notion that certain companies or institutions were so large and so interdependent and interconnected that their failure would be so disastrous and devastating that all means necessary to avoid such an outcome had to be enacted. And although the term "Too big to fail" was primarily geared to the financial sector of the US economy, it can also be applied in some cases to other sectors like construction as well.

Background: Washington, DC

It was the middle of the 1990s and the era of the MEP "rollups" was in full swing. Investors from Wall Street and other sectors of the economy felt they had the wherewithal to create an investment opportunity for both institutional and private investors by taking advantage of the inherent inefficiencies found within the fragmented construction sector of the US economy. Primarily, those inefficiencies found within MEP (mechanical, electrical, and plumbing) specialty contractors.

The consolidator's pitch at the time to both the contractors they were trying to purchase and the investors on Wall Street who would be eventually putting up the money was that larger than normal returns could be generated through the economies of scale. It also seemed at the time that consolidators felt the bigger the consolidation the better.

From the mid-1990s until the housing and "dot-com" bubbles burst in 2000, multiple consolidators went on an acquisition frenzying, competing against one another and inflating purchase prices well beyond financially sustainable levels as they continued to gobble up any and all MEP contractors willing to value their companies at many multiple times EBITDA. It was if every month during this era an announcement was being made that another specialty contractor had been purchased by someone. But then, really struck. The "dot-com" bubble burst, followed by a down turn in the economy, and the future quickly went dark as the need to hit profit and revenue growth projections each quarter anxiously took center stage.

Heavily invested in a number of "dot-com" related contracts that were abruptly put on hold, and swimming in an ocean of debt from all the inflated acquisitions, two of the largest consolidators decided that the only way to survive was to merge their respective companies. So in February 2000, a $3.6 billion publicly traded "Newco," with tens of thousands of employees on the payroll and over eleven thousand pieces of construction related equipment, became the largest facilities systems and solution provider in the US, primarily consisting of MEP contractors, with a minority number of janitorial service subsidiaries as well.

For the next year or so, the "Newco" seemed to be holding its own. Although the acquisitions of additional contractors slowed, focus turned to improving a number of the operational aspects of the large and diversified company; while simultaneously trying to curve the debt service burdening the company and making the financial statements look less attractive to the investment community. By all accounts it looked as though the merger of the two consolidators was the right decision to make going forward.

Then in June 2001, the Financial Accounting Standards Board (FASB) changed the rules for mergers and acquisitions. Companies could no longer use the pooling of interests accounting method for business combinations. Also too, companies could no longer account for mergers on their financial statements under the traditional purchase methods, which required them to amortize goodwill assets over a specific time period. In a nutshell, what this meant for consolidated companies was their already weakened financial statements that investment community was relying on got even weaker.

Like a ship taking on water, in late 2001, the "Newco" started divesting itself of all unnecessary encumbrances, including the closure of recently established branch offices; and by early 2002, the "Newco" had started the process of selling back its subsidiaries to their previous owners—all in an effort to raise cash and keep the public company afloat for as long as possible. Then, in November 2002, the "Newco" filed for bankruptcy protection.

Time for a Mental Note

Public companies are governed and regulated unlike privately held companies. From an investment perspective, public companies live and die by their financial statements, not to mention both good and bad news that helps fuel speculation. Analysts are constantly combing through the data as a means of supporting the investment community. At any given time, when changes occur in the financial statements, or, when governing regulation change, the financial impacts to a publicly traded company can be devastating, especially when companies are saddled with suffocating amounts of debt that typically will not allow ongoing operations to weather the slightest storm, let alone, survive one for any extended period of time.

Look, I'm not hung up on the fact that a business shouldn't strive to externally show a maximum amount of profit being generated from one reporting period to the next. In fact, to many like the financial services community who require it for future support, showing a profit represents a quick snapshot in time for how well, or poorly, a business might be doing. But again, this is a misguided thought process if the ultimate goal for a business is to sustain its operations from one year to the next.

My fear at this point is that given all the potential known and unknown hazards that may arise in the coming decades, current and future generations of business owners are not going to educate themselves on the lessons learned of the past, in particular the disastrous failures. Instead, future generations of business owners will be blindly trudging ahead thinking that problems will easily be solved by technology and from behind a computer screen sitting on a desk.

I can tell you this for a fact, that many businesses in the past, large and small, public and private, multigenerational, and one-time owners, who somehow lost their way for one reason or another and ultimately found themselves at the doorstep of a voluntary or involuntary liquidation, could have actually avoided their fateful outcomes had certain levels of operational performance been consistently measured, monitored, and evaluated over time. These were business owners, executive, and entrepreneurs who arrogantly thought they had what it took to navigate their way through potentially devastating commercial events, but in the end, the decisions they made didn't provide the fruit they were looking for.

Time for a Mental Note

Learning and innovation go hand in hand. The arrogance of success is to think that what you did yesterday will be sufficient for tomorrow. (William Pollard)

Yes, the managerial acumens of the past are now being revised to meet a new age of thinking. One where tech-savvy generations of new business owners, executives, and entrepreneurs will come to rely almost exclusively on technology, and, data that is called up on their personal computers or communication devices from anywhere in the world. Data that may or may not be accurate but heavily relied upon to make future decisions without regard for redundancy or a manual check and balance system to support a verification process.

It is my sincere hope that every new business owner, executive, and entrepreneur will pay heed to the trials and tribulations that many before them have gone through and learn from their stories, mistakes, and misfortunes. As we all know, there are any number of great industry sectors of the US economy that careers can be built upon; but also too, there are a great many of these industries as well that can be very unforgiving places if the terrain ahead is not closely measured, monitored, and evaluated.

8

Defining Success in Any Industry

Competent business owners, executives, and entrepreneurs recognize above all else where the security of their mere existence originates from, i.e., meeting the current and future demands of its customers. They also understand better than most that when the customer is the only source of security a business has for survival, that security must be continually earned through performance and relationship building at every level of the organization.

To have a successful company in the past, most of us were taught by experts and academia alike that business owners, executives, and entrepreneurs had to be, *better, faster, cheaper, different,* and in some cases deliver *more,* than the competition. Unfortunately, however, that's not going to be the case come post-2030 when these criteria will no longer be adequate as demographics shifts and the US economy is transformed forever.

Without question, there are countless success stories throughout multiple industries that are extremely valid. True success stories about companies whose owners had to lead their organizations through some very precarious financial and economic times, while others bravely clawed their way to the top of their respective markets defying one hurdle after another. These are the business owners worth tipping your hat to, no question.

But, defining success as a business owner is not as straightforward as one might think. Some would consider for example that whomever has a palatial home, drives nice cars, or has a significant number of luxury assets would certainly qualify to be part of a true success story. If you think this analogy is a bit far fetch, I call your attention to television shows like *Lifestyles of the Rich and Famous* or *MTV Cribs* as just two quick examples that come to mind. While other less material-minded and more pragmatic would argue that business owners who have shown time and again to be able to weather serious financial and economic storms through multiple life cycles are the ones who truly deserve the classification of being "successful." In either case, whether the perception and/or stories are true or not, most business owners will eventually find a way to convey to their competitors just how successful they really are at competing in any given marketplace.

Background: Los Angeles, CA

Remember the specialty contractor I told you about who found himself in a serious cash flow situation after his customer wanted to change the terms of their contract for work relating to a large hotel renovation? Well, there's more to the story.

I hadn't been working for the contractor for more than a month when returning to his office one day from the job site the contractor told me this story about the success of one of his contractor friends who had recently retired after scoring huge profits off a very large project. I'm not exactly sure how the conversation started in the first place, but out of the blue here comes this story about an unrelated third party contractor's success in the construction industry.

The story started out by the contractor describing the attributes of his colleague in hyper-admirable terms, one of which was the fact that his colleague was able to get a very successful business established in a reasonably short amount of time. As the story continued, the contractor told me that his colleague was able to develop a strong cadre of field supervisors and a nucleus of good craftsmen to install his work—two aspects of contracting every successful contractor works to achieve during their business's life cycle. Additional attributes of his colleague included terms like savvy, smart, moderate risk-taker—as if these were the only characteristics that embodied every contractor aspiring to be a success one day.

Then, the story turned to a mega-project his colleague had been awarded a few years back. The contractor explained in some detail how his colleague went about setting up the project and ultimately delivering it to his customer. Basically, in the contractor's opinion, it was nothing short of a masterful performance by his colleague and his company, and one to be emulated for decades to come.

As the contractor was wrapping up the story, I noticed his facial expression starting to change a bit. Grinning from ear to ear, the contractor said in a euphoric voice that the mega-project had made his colleague so much money due to all of the change orders being generated throughout the course of the project that once the project was completed his colleague decided to shut the doors and retire.

It would be years later when I was reflecting back on this time in my career and this particular story that it dawned on me that there existed an ironic correlation between the "so-called" success story told by the contractor I worked for at the time and what eventually happened to him and his contracting business less than a decade later.

On the surface, stories like the one just told would most likely qualify to some like-minded business owners as a true success story. But what I find peculiar when listening to these types of stories is the fact that often times the story teller, whether it's the business owner or a colleague, is more interested in the outcome then the journey itself. For example, in the story just told, the business owner's colleague, who personally reaped the benefits of a "windfall" profit from the mega-project, in no way could have delivered the project on his own, but yet, he is the one, not the company as a whole, who comes away with the glorious reputation for being a successful business owner.

Time for a Mental Note

In order to successfully deliver a construction project, contractors have an entire complement of employees who deal with personnel, inventory, and cash flow requirements every single day. As a means for delivering a mega-project like the one described in the contractor's success story, the contractor's colleague would have needed a whole host of support staff in the office, along with over 100 craftspeople in the field performing the actual work. Moreover, you will also remember, according to the contractor telling the story, that his colleague had a very successful operation before he landed the mega-project, which would have meant, the company would have also had to have additional employees managing that work as well. One could easily speculate that over two hundred employees (and by extension their families), if not more, had a stake in delivering the mega-project to the ultimate benefit of the contractor's colleague.

When you think about it, given all the risks a business owner, e.g., contractor, takes on a daily basis, why shouldn't they toot their own horn from time to time?

In a lot of ways, succeeding in any risky business like construction contracting is a lot like the euphoria a mountain climber feels each time he or she reaches a certain stage, or camp, as they ascend Mt. Everest. Not only do they stop to take a well-deserved rest and reflect on the accomplishment they just completed, but they also take the time to acclimate themselves to a different environment prior to moving on. An environment that can become very seductive if not held in check, and one that could lead to taking on more risk that may or may not be advisable given certain circumstances.

I use the metaphor of climbing Mt. Everest to being a business owner because it's important for you, the reader, to understand the unbelievable challenges that face business owners on a regular basis as they attempt to successfully navigate their way through an ever-changing economy. Like the difficulties of climbing Mt. Everest, certain industries, like the construction industry, are no easy place to make a living, especially for unqualified or undisciplined business owners who allow external perceptions and internal desires guide their behavior and decision making processes.

In Stephen Covey's 1988 best seller, *The 7 Habits of Highly Effective People*, the very first habit Mr. Covey discusses is the concept of: "Be Proactive." Mr. Covey goes on to explain that those who behave in a manner opposite of proactive people, i.e., reactive people, more times than not will allow themselves to be affected by their physical environment. This in turn, affects how people behave, perform, and/or react to certain stimuli, including environmental challenges. In other words, reactive people believe they have limited choices in response to particular stimuli, and as a result, narrow their concentration to the one or two things they feel need to be influenced the most at any given time. For example, getting to the top of Mt. Everest at any cost as opposed to making sure you as a climber take the necessary precautions along the way in order to give yourself the best chance possible of actually reaching the summit.

In life, as in business, short-term thinking, i.e., being reactive, is a reenforced mind-set, as is long-term thinking, i.e., being proactive. If you are a short-term thinking business owner, your thought processes, and subsequent actions, are most likely governed by what's called the "Scarcity Mentality," i.e., grab what you can while you can and protect it from those who you perceive might want to take it away because there's simply not enough of it to go around for everyone. As a result, people guided by the "Scarcity Mentality" harbor the belief that most things in life are governed by limitations, and because of this, it's perfectly acceptable to be selfish instead of being generous to others.

To have the "scarcity mentality" as a business owner heading into the next two generational life cycles of owning or operating a business, post—2030, is not the mind-set to have if you plan to be successful, and here's why.

The "scarcity mentality" alone can be a powerful driving force behind opposing parties constantly competing against one another; and although many industries don't necessarily foster a "kill or be killed" environment like in the coliseum days, the vast majority of business owners operating today actually do resemble having a gladiator's mind-set. A mind-set that will not serve them well going forward even if they make it past the next generational life cycle of their respective business.

Compelled to compete, "scarcity minded" business owners are by choice, simply unable to broaden their perspective on what truly matters to a business purpose, i.e., meeting the future demands of customers. As tunnel vision and paranoia sets in, competition for "scarcity minded" business owners becomes a very narrow way of life that is all consuming—requiring them to constantly be looking over their shoulder each and every day for what the competition might be doing, or saying, to set themselves apart from the rest of the pack. A paranoia that is so prevalent and controlling at times that some business owners will actually embrace a metaphoric "kill or be killed" attitude, stooping to unprecedented levels of decorum and incivility at the ultimate expense of long-term sustainability.

Time for a Metal Note

"The 'secret sauce' to Amazon's success is an 'obsessive compulsive focus' on customer over competitor." (Jeff Bezos)

Without a shadow of doubt, business owners possessing the "Scarcity Mentality" post-2030 are doomed long before they even know it. Post-2030, looking over one's shoulder is the last place a business owner wants to find him or herself with all the shifting demographics and changes in technology yet to be introduced to the US economy. In fact, highly qualified business owners, executives, and entrepreneurs today, running "high performance" operations, will emphatically tell you that the need to be focused on the future far outweighs any need to spend time lamenting about the past if they want to survive another generational business life cycle in the US.

I cannot stress enough times throughout this book, how destructive the "scarcity mentality" has been to a company's ongoing operation, or, to industries like the construction industry as a whole. Instead of business owners, executives, and entrepreneurs channeling their energies each and every day toward measuring, monitoring, and evaluating performance metrics within their own operations (performance metrics critically vital to sustaining a company's liquidity and long-term sustainability), "scarcity mentality" business owners have found it more rewarding to channel those same energies through an increasingly narrow prism of what it is they think defines their potential success as a business owner regardless of the toll it may take on (a) their own business's operation, (b) their company's reputation, or (c) the community they serve.

Background: Phoenix, AZ

Living in Los Angeles at the time and having gone to Arizona State (ASU) studying nuclear engineering, my career goal was to always get back to the Phoenix area someday. It's an awesome place to visit and live, and I highly recommend people taking the time to go there for the experience.

One day, I received a call about a medium-sized contracting firm in Phoenix who was looking to fill a project manager/estimator position in order to support their ever expanding backlog of work. The company was advertised to have a very progressive owner who had only been in business for about eight years, but was quickly making a competitive name for himself throughout the construction market.

So I made the call to the contractor's office to see if the position was still available, and it was.

The next day, I faxed off my resume to a person they designated and followed up shortly thereafter with a phone call to insure they had received it. I was told by the contractor's assistant that she had in fact received my resume, and that the owner of the company would be in contact with me as soon as he had some spare time. My immediate thought was that since there was a current opening at the company, the owner would be calling me back within a day or two—or so I thought.

Day 1 goes by and no call, day 2 goes by and no call, and finally on day 3, I decide to place another call to the contractor's office inquiring about his availability. This time I was told that the contractor was preoccupied on another project, but I was assured that he would be interviewing me by either phone or in person very soon. Later that same day, I receive a call back from the owner himself.

The owner apologized for not getting back with me sooner, but said he had been spending a considerable amount of time away from the office on another project. He then said, he would be back in touch with me in a couple of days to set up a time for me to visit with him in Phoenix where we could discuss things in more depth. Somewhat relieved by the contractor's reassurance, I stopped fretting over the whole prospect of the situation for the next few days.

Then, the cycle of waiting and anticipation started all over again.

After about a week of waiting, I decided to force the issue once again. I called the contractor's office, and like the numerous times before his assistant said he was not in. However, this time I told his assistant that I was planning a trip to the Phoenix area within the next week to see some old college buddies and wanted to know if the contractor would be available for me to come by and visit with him. She replied that she would have to check with him and his availability because at present he was rarely in the office for any extended length of time. I then thought to myself, if the owner of the company is away so much, surely there has to be someone else in charge that I could talk to about the position, but there wasn't, the owner was it.

Later that day, I received a call back from the contractor's assistant who said the owner could meet with me on such and such a day at such and such a time.

As the interview unfolded the owner could not have been more gracious, to the point of being very apologetic for his untimely responses. He reiterated again that he had been preoccupied for the past several months on a challenging project. I then noticed as he was telling me this that the owner had gotten a peculiar grin on his face.

Sensing something was off about this challenging project, I asked, "What were some of the challenges you were having to deal with?" He again smiled and started to explain the reality of the situation.

As it turned out, after all this time of being away from the office, the so-called "challenging project" wasn't a company related project after all. The owner was actually spending most, if not all, of his waking hours overseeing the design and construction of his new palatial home being built in a residential area at the base of a mountain range.

Believe it or not, it's just not stories about a business owner's preoccupation with building a luxury home at the base of a mountain, or on top of a mountain as some have done, that takes a business owner's attention away from the short-term and long-term obligations of the company. It's also stories about business owners getting preoccupied with ancillary things like (a) running for public office; (b) owning part of a professional sports franchise; (c) holding time consuming positions with industry associations; (d) dabbling in real estate and real estate development; (e) owning hotels, resorts, and adventure camps; (f) buying restaurant franchises or starting their own restaurant; (g) investing in high-end cattle breeding operations; or (h) buying, breeding, and showing exotic animals—just to name of few of the more popular and well-known ones that have been around industries like construction for quite some time.

Call it a phenomenon or human nature, but I have seen time and time again throughout my career that for whatever reason when business owners of small or medium sized companies get to a certain size, they instinctively start thinking to themselves: "Okay! I'm now a successful businessman (or woman), so I'm going to go off and enjoy the fruits of my labor and let the company start running itself." Then, as if like clockwork, the adverse effects of absentee management kicks in and the previously well-established company begins to fail.

Obviously, not all business owners look at the "risk scale" from the same perspective. Some business owners are extremely risk adverse, meaning they spend more of their time and money avoiding risky situations than dealing with actual risks head on. On the other hand, there are some business owners who have a very high tolerance for risk, employing the motto, "Nothing ventured, nothing gained." But without exception, regardless of the level of risk tolerance a business owner may possess, especially in industries like construction, every major decision must first make the journey between "greed" and "fear."

"Greed" tells business owners, particularly those having a "scarcity mentality," to take all they can when they can, while "Fear" tells a business owner to be on the lookout for anything that could possibly cause them to lose it all. One minute the emotional pendulum swings toward a downturn in the economy and potentially tough times ahead—i.e., "fear," and the business owner starts thinking that it's time to immediately start limiting his or her exposure going forward. Then, at some point, the economy turns positive and the emotional pendulum suddenly swings back the opposite direction where "windfall" profits are certainly on the horizon and life is all well and good again, i.e., "greed."

As you have read in previous chapters, most business owners today, particularly ones with the "scarcity mentality," are driven solely be profit, revenue growth, and status. They are consumed each day with looking over their shoulder hoping that every tomorrow will be better, but no worse, than the day before. It will be these business owners who will struggle to survive as the decades ahead unfold.

Time for a Mental Note

Long-term thinking is governed by what's called the "abundance mentality," where thoughts are re-enforced by the fact that there's plenty of resources, opportunities, and successes to go around for everyone so long as there is a willingness to work for it. Needless to say, business owners of "*high performance*" companies have this particular mentality.

As I close out this chapter I want to leave every business owner, executive, and entrepreneur with this reality check as the transformative decade of 2030 approaches. Sound business models of the past, based on conventional wisdom and brought forward by previous generations, will eventually become extinct over time. I say this because there is absolutely no question in my mind that "reactive," complacent, and yes, "scarcity mentality," business owners will be replaced in the coming years by more tech-savvy, forward thinking, "*high performance*" companies. Companies, who no longer relying on the past, but rather those who are already preparing to face the challenges of the next fifty years, and beyond, by addressing:

a) Lingering skilled and unskilled labor shortages that have been plaguing industries since before the turn of the twenty-first century

b) Increased language barriers created by the mass amount of international immigration that has occurred since the 1980s

c) Stresses on the US financial system caused by extremely high levels of federal, state, and local municipality debt that's been accumulated since before the turn of the twenty-first century

d) Generational gaps created by an aging US population that is living and working longer as the digital age continues to expand, improve, and impact how people live and work

e) An industry moving quickly toward automation, modularization, and pre-fabricated assemblies of components

f) Social media's impact on a business's reputation, customer development skills, employment hiring practices, and a whole host of other business related items and concepts

For the business owners and executives with a pedigree of being performance based, consumed each day with making sure they maintain the necessary level of operational alignment, synergy, and liquidity in order to meet certain standards of performance, the future US economy will certainly be a very challenging but rewarding time. By constantly measuring, monitoring, and evaluating every strategic aspect of an operation, while at the same time laying the foundation for subsequent generational life cycles to succeed, wealth and prosperity certainly lies ahead.

A New Brand of Leadership

For decades, we have all been taught through the halls of academia that in order for a business to thrive and prosper it must first establish and then maintain a hierarchical management structure focused solely on maximizing the effectiveness of superior/subordinate relationships. And because of this paradigm, most business owners, executives, entrepreneurs, and employees will tell you that they do not see themselves as being anything other than "reactive" participants to the current demands of their customers. Which is also why, most businesses in the US are based solely on managing previously established processes passed down from one generation of employees to another while ignoring innovations that can change the future. Unless of course you're a tech company.

So why is it that most non-tech business owners, executives and entrepreneurs share the importance of this paradigm?

Up until the late 1970s, the US economy was powered by a strong manufacturing base and union workforce primarily centered in the Midwest, upper Midwest, and Northeast. Then as the 1980s came along, two important events started to happen in the US: (a) new service based sectors of the US economy started to emerge with the advent of the tech revolution, and (b) older generations started migrating to the south and west, embracing a warmer climate and lower costs of living. All the while, developing countries in Asia like

Japan, China, and South Korea, with their low wages and need to become economically sustainable, quietly and methodically started to expand their manufacturing base.

Then in early 1992, the governments of US, Mexico, and Canada ratified a trade agreement called NAFTA, which in turn decimated the manufacturing base in the US for decades to come. But there's something else that happened to the US economy that without question transformed its socioeconomic direction forever. It was the desire of older generations to see their children go to college.

In 1965, the year most would agree was the start of Generation X, there were approximately 6 million students enrolled in higher education curriculums. Fifteen short years later, in 1980, that number had doubled to just over 12 million. Now add Generation Y to the discussion, where in 2010 over 21 million students were enrolled in higher education.

Arguably, for the past three decades, whether older generational leaders will acknowledge it or not, industries throughout the US economy have begrudgingly allowed technology to complement their well-established investments in the "bricks and mortar," paper-based, manual aspect of business related operations for fear that someone, qualified or not, may lose their job to a more productive, cost effective means of procurement and installation. Some blame the unions for not relinquishing their grip in time on failing industries. Others blame it on unreliable and unproven technologies. But regardless of the excuses or reasons, this very fact alone should give every business owner, executive, and entrepreneur pause to consider what the consequences could be starting around the year 2030 if barriers do not start getting taken down sooner rather than later in order to allow a more productive work environment utilizing advancements in technology and innovative systems.

It's a fact, and one that other generational leaders are going to have to come to grips with, younger generations don't see the world the same way as previous generations do. Younger generations are better educated, not necessarily wiser, and are far more tech savvy than older generations. And because the US is educating both domestic and international students alike, it's a given that the world's populations are getting better educated and more technologically advanced as well. Which in the end means the US has no other choice but to keep up with the rest of the world, technologically speaking, or it will no longer be able to relish in the spotlight of being the industrial and commercial powerhouse it is today.

So prepare yourself, the business owners, executives, and entrepreneurs of tomorrow are definitely going to look and sound very different than what previous generations of traditional business owners, executives and entrepreneurs have been used to. The days of Armani suits, full Windsor knot ties, and Ferragamo shoes in the board rooms will slowly be phased out for more socially acceptable, and arguably more comfortable, Crewneck T-shits, jeans, and tennis shoes; not to mention seeing an occasional tattoo and/or body piercing from time to time. Say what?

Yep, you can take it to the bank when I tell you that the well-established traditions and values established by previous generations in the past are quickly giving way to new socially acceptable norms where comfort, convenience, and an open tolerance to personal diversification is becoming more commonplace. So much so, that business owners and executives of companies, large and small, are rewriting the book on leadership and how best to guide their organizations in a tech-driven environment.

The cultural environments being created by Generations X and Y leaders today are ones that are constantly looking for ways to empower and inspire each and every employee within the organizational structure. Cultures first of giving, then of taking.

Look at *Fortunes' 2017 100 Best* for example and ask yourself this question:

What is it that makes a company like Google be at the top of the list for six years in row?

The answer comes in two parts:

a) From an emotional perspective, its luxury perks that Google provides its employees like: free gourmet food, haircuts, and laundry service. Not to mention a much appreciated parental-leave policies, openness to diversity and internal causes of its employees, support of transgender workers, and workshops that help foster a safe and inclusive workplace.

b) From an operational perspective, it's their executive leadership's ability to convey policies and procedures to their employees in such a way that operational alignment, synergy, and liquidity automatically takes precedence over any operational dispute that may break out from time to time. And because Google's business purpose is so well known amongst all of its employees, it alone inherently acts as the company's perpetual arbitrator, resolving differing points of view long before any particular dispute can escalate.

Time for a Mental Note

This from Stephen R. Covey's *The 7 Habits of Highly Effective People,* "Habit 6: Synergy":

> *To put it simply, synergy means "two heads are better than one." Synergize is the habit of creative cooperation. It is teamwork, open-mindedness, and the adventure of finding new solutions to old problems. But it doesn't just happen on its own. It's a process, and through that process, people bring all their personal experience and expertise to the table. Together, they can produce far better results that they could individually. Synergy lets us discover jointly things we are much less likely to discover by ourselves. It is the idea that the whole is greater than the sum of the parts. One plus one equals three, or six, or sixty--you name it.*
>
> *When people begin to interact together genuinely, and they're open to each other's influence, they begin to gain new insight. The capability of*

inventing new approaches is increased exponentially because of differences.

Valuing differences is what really drives synergy. Do you truly value the mental, emotional, and psychological differences among people? Or do you wish everyone would just agree with you so you could all get along? Many people mistake uniformity for unity; sameness for oneness. One word--boring! Differences should be seen as strengths, not weaknesses. They add zest to life.

One of the very first things you have to understand about performance based companies is that they perpetually cultivate throughout their organizational structure a very distinctive attitude that outwardly expresses a passion toward excellence in everything they do (Apple and Steve Jobs should immediately come to mind). An attitude (culture) that is derived from strong executive leadership who constantly demand an internal discipline of exceptional performance that inherently promotes: (a) operational, synergy and liquidity; (b) innovation and customer dependency; (c) employee interdependency; (d) community service and involvement; (e) continuous process improvement; and (f) a safe, equitable, and diversified work environment for all employees.

As reasonable and logical as all that may sound, you may be surprised to learn that the vast majority of companies throughout the US, and the world for that matter, have never adopted it, and in a number of cases, still resisting it. Why you say? Because if profit and revenue growth are not the main focus of any internal discussion, nothing else really matters to their leadership. Don't believe me?

In the December 25, 2017/January 1, 2018, issue of ENR, under the caption "Executive News," one of the largest construction companies in the world announced the promotion of one of their seasoned executives to the position of global CEO after spending nearly a year shoring up the company's US operations. Why the needed change at the top? Because of the company's "failure to consistently meet profitability expectations."

The article then went onto say that "Improving profitability on more selectively chosen contracts will be a key focus"; which according to the article will be achieved through an improved bid risk-management process and a call for an industry-wide "shift to a more disciplined approach toward bidding." In other words, the company believes that profitability will once again be achieved through: (a) a better selection process of projects to pursue; and (b) the accuracy in which each project will be bid (which is code for how much profit the company can add to the accumulative costs of a bid at bid time), and not through meeting performance metrics month in and month out that can achieve and maintain an effective operational alignment, synergy, and liquidity of all business units and operations. Roughly eight months later after the article was published, surprise, surprise, the same company reported profit write-down of $100 million stemming from two large projects in the US, plus, a $44 million goodwill impairment charge.

I'll say it again. The ultimate goal of executive leadership should always be to cultivate a culture that inherently focuses every employee's attention on the need to achieve and maintain a level of operational alignment, synergy, and liquidity that meets the short-term and long-term obligations of the company. An outcome that can only occur through the constant pursuit and achievement of higher levels of operational performance. As higher levels of operational performance are achieved, only then can business owners, executives, and entrepreneurs expect to see marginal benefits, i.e., returns, being generated at *sustainable* levels from one financial reporting period to the next.

Time for a Mental Note

This from Stephen R. Covey's *Principle-Centered Leadership* relating to "Organizational Alignment":

> *In the future, systems reengineering will not be enough. Excellent customer service will not be enough. Manufacturing defect-free products to specifications will not be enough. The future is now.*

The enduring, empowering high-performance organization of the future will require total organizational alignment to foster innovation, nurture continuous improvement and sustain total quality results. Leaders, managers and employees at every level will need a holistic, integrated paradigm of what your organization is all about, the dynamic environment in which it operates and an accurate understanding of how all the complex elements of your organizational ecosystem work together.

The principle of alignment means working together in harmony, going in the same direction, supporting each other. Total organizational alignment means that within the realities of the surrounding environment, all components of your organization-including your mission, vision, values, strategy, structure, systems, individual style and skills, and especially the minds and hearts of your people-support and work together effectively for maximum performance. It is a process that never ends.

For obvious reasons, it is unreasonable to consider that a business owner or entrepreneur would ever plan to build his or her own personal fortune by investing in a non-sustainable business that only operates, and potentially creates, a profit one day at a time. But you know what, that's exactly what a number of business owners and entrepreneurs do each and every day when they only seek to know (in a vacuum if you will) the level of profit a product or service is generating their company at any given time.

If you really want to know the secrets behind how the leadership of "high performance" companies avoid the devastating pitfalls of their respective industries while maintaining higher levels of operational alignment, synergy, and liquidity, this is how:

a)   The leadership of "high performance" companies always lead by example

b) The leadership of "high performance" companies inspire others to follow by embracing the concept of "servant leadership"—shifting the culture away from managing for results, i.e., profits, and more toward designing and creating cultural environments that generate sustainable levels of profit through interdependency and operational alignment.

c) The leadership of "high performance" companies stay in constant communications with the entire organization, passionately promoting to everyone: (a) "Why" it is the company is in business to begin with; (b) "What" it is they believe in; (c) the importance of operational alignment, synergy, and liquidity, i.e., a culture of interdependency; and (d) customer and community development/involvement.

d) The leadership of "high performance" companies are on the constant look out for good employees needing additional training and improvement that in the end will provide them the ability to add value to the organization beyond their being recognized as just being good employees.

e) The leadership of "high performance" companies constantly show a profound trust and confidence in their managers and supervisors, not only to make the "right" decisions each and every day, but to be discreet with sensitive information.

f) The leadership of "high performance" companies create cross collaborative organizational structures, along with systems of accountability, in order to ensure that no individual, no group, no department, no division, and no branch within the organization are allowed to operate under a self-governing independence.

g) The leadership of "high performance" companies continually strive to set stretch goals for their managers and supervisors in an effort to improve current levels of performance. It's a philosophy that says in effect: "Yesterday's achievements are now the baseline for which tomorrow's goals will be measured against."

To maintain their elite status as a "high performance" company, business owners, executives, and entrepreneurs constantly stay focused on creating synergy through their own unique leadership fundamentals. As blocking and tackling fundamentals are to coaching a championship football team, so too are the following operational fundamentals of "high performance" companies:

a) constantly measuring, monitoring, and evaluating processes in order to achieve ever-changing standards of performance

b) utilizing process controls and mapping in order to break down organizational activities to a micro level, i.e., benchmarking

c) effectively communicating with employees at all levels of the organization

d) constantly identifying the complexity of any process in order to attack and complete the more difficult tasks at hand in the most time-efficient manner

e) establishing and achieving stretch goals

f) creating strategies and tactics for getting ahead, and staying ahead, of the competition

g) constantly monitoring any potential impact to an established succession program

h) constantly evaluating employee performance, and making the appropriate adjustments accordingly

i) requiring employees to balance their work and private lives

Without question, business owners, executives, and entrepreneurs of "high performance" companies have a much broader spectrum of fundamentals, managerial tools, and performance metrics to help guide them from one generational life cycle to the next. They recognize better than most that to be a successful leader in business it is imperative that they at their core have the ability to actually lead those who are willing to follow no matter which generation they were born in in order for the company to survive well beyond industry standards for longevity.

Customer Loyalty: The Holy Grail of Business Purpose

In any business venture, a company must have the ability to sell a product or service to a willing buyer; otherwise, no one in the company will have anything to do. Seems like a pretty straight forward proposition. Right?

All great business owners, executives, entrepreneurs and salesmen understand the concept of selling better than most. They get it! They know it really doesn't matter if a company has (a) the best product on the market, (b) the highest level of customer service and satisfaction before and after a product or service is sold, (c) uses the highest quality of material, or (d) has the leanest/most efficient production processes. If someone is unwilling to buy a product or service, there's really no reason to be in business in the first place.

Time for a Mental Note

"There is only one valid definition of business purpose: to create a customer." (Peter F. Drucker)

But what every great business owner, executive, entrepreneur and salesman also knows is that just because a customer buys from a seller once, doesn't mean he or she will ever be back to buy a second or third time. Why?

Think about it this way. Put yourself in the shoes of the executive who is out of town on a business trip. Its eight forty-five at night when you receive a call from your distraught wife returning home from a night out at the movies with your teenage daughter. In a voice filled with panic your wife informs you that she's parked on the side of a major interstate with a flat tire. It's raining out and there is absolutely no ways she's getting out of the car and changing the tire with interstate traffic speeding by on wet pavement.

Feeling a strong sense of anxiety, you immediately determine their location and start calling tire stores in the area to see if they can send someone to help.

The first tire store you call informs you that they were just closing up for the evening, but if you were to call back in the morning they would be happy to put your service call to the top of the list for an immediate response.

The second tire store you try automatically takes you to a nationwide call center and instructs you to go through a series of prompts. By the time you get to the last prompt, you hear an electronic voice on the other end of the line informing you that the store has closed for the evening.

Desperately trying to get some help for your wife and daughter, you try a third tire store. The call is immediately answered by a gentlemen's voice who politely asks, "How may I help you?" You immediately explain your situation, and even though he informs you that he was just about to close up for the night, he replies in calm, reassuring voice, "Don't worry, we'll take care of them."

After giving the gentleman on the phone the location of the car and your wife's cell phone number, you contact your wife and let her know that help is on the way.

Two hours later, you get a call from a very thankful wife telling you in a very relieved voice that she's at home with your daughter safe and sound. She then tells you that she was surprised to learn that all the tire store charged her for the service was the replacement of the tire and nothing else.

Six months go by, and you notice that one of your cars need a new set of tires. Who do you think you're going to call or go see first even though you know you might be paying a little more by not shopping other tire stores in the area?

Believe it or not, although many would have you believe that "customer satisfaction" is what brings customers back time and again to buy your products, it's really not. What truly brings customers back time and again is an emotional connection created by an individual's own "Value" system. A "Value" system that had been pretty well developed by the age of ten, and locked in by the age of twenty. "Values" that people possess based on sex, age, and ethnicity that direct a buyer's behavior. For business owners, executives, and entrepreneurs of the future, this is a critical part of any business purpose to know and understand.

Time for a Mental Note

Today, most businesses in the US are still owned and operated by members of the Silent and Baby Boomer Generations; and although these two generations harbor strikingly different "Value" systems in some cases, they both hold true to the conservative side of moderate, hard work, and a willingness to tell people exactly what's on their mind. As you have read in previous chapters, such is not the case when it comes to the "value" systems being held near and dear to members of Generations X and Y.

As neuroscientists continue to study how the chemicals of the brain effects human behavior, it's interesting to note that researchers have found a direct correlation being how, what, and from whom consumers buy relative to the emotions being transmitted in the brain at the time of purchase. One neuroscientist in particular has argued that mirror neurons in the brain help humans understand the actions and intentions of other humans. Moreover, the same neuroscientist has argued that mirror neurons aid in a human's capacity for a range of emotions such as empathy; which in short is the ability of one human being to understand and share the feelings of another. So why is this important to future business owners, executives, and entrepreneurs?

Neuroscientists know that people consistently buy things based on emotions, memories, and herd instincts, not to mention a variety of other minor reasons. But the key to most buying, or spending if you will, all comes down to one thing, one's desire to do so. For example, if an object, product or service, is one of perceived desire by a buyer, and is somehow related to an emotion, memory, or herd instinct, triggers in the brain immediately go off for the sole purpose of acquiring the object. In other words, if a buyer has a strong emotional attachment to a seller, or, remembers an event(s) that conjures up positive thoughts and/or emotions about the seller, the buyer will most likely buy from that one particular seller over and over again as opposed to someone else that the buyer has no attachment to.

Background: Los Angeles, CA

Remember from an earlier chapter I told the story of a medium sized contractor who got into trouble after agreeing to a contract for the electrical work on a historic hotel renovation in downtown Los Angeles, and one day he received a call from the owner/developer asking for a meeting to be held the Monday before Thanksgiving? And at that meeting the owner/developer announced that they were exercising the "Termination for Convenience" clause in the contract, and, that the medium sized contractor with all one hundred or so electricians working on site had seventy-two hours to vacate the property of all personnel, tools, and equipment. Here's the rest of the story:

You will recall that what started this whole chain of events in the first place was the overall budget for the owner/developer started getting severely strained once the final design and scope of work had been determined. And because of their anticipated shortfall in funding the entire project, the owner/developer asked the major subcontractors (particularly the MEP contractors) on the project to renegotiate the terms of their agreement. Unfortunately, the lone holdout was the electrical contractor I worked for at the time.

As time continued to march on without any substantive feedback from the electrical contractor on whether or not he would renegotiate the terms of the contract, the owner/developer was left with no choice but to immediately start looking for a replacement contractor. And as it turns out, the first call that was made by the owner/developer was to the second runner to see if he would be interested in taking over the project.

Projects the size and scope of the massive hotel renovation catches the eye of many folks from the construction industry, and a large electrical contractor in the area happened to be one of them. A contractor who was also no stranger to the importance of spending the necessary time and resources on building lasting relationships with current potential customers.

Armed with a number of recreational assets at his disposal, the owner of the company would often times look to his prized luxury yacht moored in a nearby harbor where he would host lavish gatherings for customers and dignitaries a like. It was at one of these lavish gatherings on board the luxury yacht that the owner/developer of the massive renovation project got to know the competing contractor; and where the seeds for a future relationship became securely planted.

Although unsuccessful at being awarded the contract for the hotel renovation project, the competing contractor and owner/developer stayed in touch with one another in the hopes of working together on another project in the future. Approximately eighteen months later, when the conversation with the existing electrical contractor deteriorated, the owner/developer did not hesitate to call the competing contractor to see if he would still be interested in the project. And as they say, the rest is history.

Future business owners, executives, and entrepreneurs who attempting to meet the future demands of their customers must always remember that every individual's behavior is defined by what does and does not have "Value" to them. What's even more critical to know is that by nature's own design, we as humans are all creatures of desire, where good always trumps bad. Things that are considered to be good to people, create "value," and things that are considered to be bad to people, destroy "value." It's as simple as that.

So what are some of the good things people still have an emotional attachment to and therefore a desire to pay large sums of money? How about…(a) listening to Beatles or Elvis songs, (b) attending Star Trek conventions, (c) owning a '57 Chevy and other vintage automobiles, (d) collecting old baseball cards and memorabilia, or (e) faithfully rooting for their favorite sports franchise like the Boston Red Sox or Chicago Cubs. All of these things are considered good in the hearts and minds of many, so to a buyer they have "value." Hence the term "sentimental value."

Understanding that human desire dictates how money is used and/or spent is the first step in selling a product or service to a potential customer. That said, the reverse is also true, money in no way dictates or influence a person's desire; which explains why "customer loyalty," or a customer's willingness to continually buy the same brand over and over again regardless of known intangibles, has absolutely nothing to with a customer being satisfied with a product or service. If you don't believe that, than why have so many bikers stuck with riding Harleys for so many years, even after years of oil leaking out of them like a sieve? Or, why do so many sports fans shell out thousands of dollars each year to support their favorite professional sports franchise, even though the team consistently loses games year in and year out? Here's why!

Take the New York professional sports franchise market from a major league baseball fan's perspective. In New York, at the professional level, you have one of two choices, either the Yankees or the Mets, one from the American League the other from the National League.

The Yankees have won twenty-seven World Championships, and consistently have the highest or second highest payroll of any competing franchise. They arguably have some of the best ballplayers in the league, and typically provide their fans with great baseball year in and year out. In 2009, the Yankees rewarded their fans with a brand new state of the art $2.3 billion stadium with a seating capacity of 52,325. But with the Yankees franchise there's only one major problem, selling out home games during the regular season is not a seldom occurrence.

By comparison, let's take a look at the Boston professional sports franchise market from a major league baseball fan's perspective as well. A short four-hour drive up Interstate 95.

In Boston, you have one choice, the Red Sox, who happen to be the archrivals of the Yankees. The Red Sox have won only 9 World Championships, and are typically just behind the Yankees when it comes to the total salaries paid to their players. The Red Sox also still play baseball at Fenway Park which was built in 1912, and has a seating capacity of 37,305.

So far, commercial advantage go to the Yankees.

In 2016, New York had an estimated metropolitan area population of roughly 20 million people, Boston on the other hand had 4.7 million (a factor of four times). Medium income difference between the two cities was about $7,000 per year (New York being higher), which is about the equivalent of a single season ticket price.

Still, commercial advantage go to the Yankees.

Now by comparison, one could easily conclude that the Yankees have a competitive advantage over the Red Sox since they have so much more to offer in terms of population density and monetary fan support. But interestingly enough, the Red Sox: (a) consistently sell out every home game during the season; (b) consistently have the most expensive average ticket price in the league; and (c) consistently finish in the top three markets for ticket sales of all MLB franchises. Why? Because they have one thing most other professional sports franchises don't have, a loyal fan base that has long surpassed the test of time.

So how can this be? What creates this phenomenon in Boston that the New York Yankees would dearly love to possess? Why do customers (fans) keeping coming back year after year in Boston, and at times, willing to pay more money for the product or service compared to other sports franchises even though the Red Sox very seldom win a World Series title? In fact, the Red Sox had a stretch of 86 consecutive years where they didn't win a single World Series title but still sold out home games year after year.

The answers to these questions are the same answers as if they were asked about competing businesses in a given market. "Loyalty."

Loyalty, or the act of someone being loyal, is commonly defined as an expression created in response to an originating act, expression, or perception of some kind, i.e., an exchange if you will. Remember the hypothetical story I told in an earlier chapter about the business-man being away on a trip and his panic wife called with a flat tire on the side of rain slick interstate?

Loyalty can be created from both positive and negative acts, expressions, and perceptions. Take the generations of loyal fans that follow the band, The Grateful Dead, a.k.a. the Dead, from one concert venue to the next. Why is that? It's because bands like The Grateful Dead go the extra mile to give back to their fan base in just about everything they do. For example:

a) It is the Dead's desire to allow fans to tape their performances, while other bands make it a point to hire extra security to track down tapings and destroy fan's recording equipment, all the while passing along those extra costs to their fans through higher ticket prices. The Dead, on the other hand, go out of their way to set up designated areas so that fans wanting to tape the music could achieve the best sound to record.

b) In order for the Dead to make their fans part of their culture, they actively participate and encourage the trading and sharing of T-shirts and other memorabilia before every show. By contrast, other big name bands have security guards walk the parking lots in search of unauthorized or unofficial T-shirts and merchandise being sold in order to stop it, which typically ends with violators getting kicked off the lot.

c) After the Dead caught wind that promoters were gauging their fans with inflated prices they decided to take over the process themselves in order to keep ticket prices as low as possible.

If you were to ask band members "why" they felt it was necessary to be so involved with their fan base, most would tell you that it wasn't just about the money. For them it's all about a traveling community that encompasses both the band itself and the legends of fans that follow them from one venue to the next. To the Dead, if they can show they care about the fans, the fans should respond in kind. As a result, a bond and strong sense of loyalty gets created.

Obviously, some in the sports entertainment and music industries get it. They've figured out that in order to create a loyal fan base, they first have to get the relationship to a one-on-one personal level. The same is also true for any business and the communities they serve. If business owners, executives, and entrepreneurs desire "Loyalty" from a customer base through good times and bad, they must first show, or express, a willingness to extend a goodwill gesture before any meaningful and unconditional transaction can occur.

Background: Phoenix, AZ

Remember the story I told from an earlier chapter about a contractor who had spent months away from the office designing and building a new luxury home at the base of mountain? Did I also mention he was absolutely phenomenal when it came to marketing and business development?

The year was 1977 when the industrial service electrician decided to move to the Phoenix area with his family and opened his own electrical contracting business. Joined by an estimator colleague, the two started pursuing small work throughout the area with the hopes of growing the company into something larger and more formidable in the coming years.

It was now the middle to late 1980s, when the Phoenix metropolitan area construction market was literally booming. The population growth was expanding so rapidly that people would say as they drove by a vacant lot traveling through the city and suburbs, "That lot won't be vacant much longer… I wonder what someone will be building there?"

Contractors of all disciplines, along with entrepreneurs throughout the country, were aware the news about how great the growth prospects were for the foreseeable future in the Phoenix area; and most of whom were more than willing to relocate their operations, or at the very least, expand them to the valley of the sun.

One of the contractors based in the Midwest who was willing to expand its operations to the Phoenix area in 1984 was a family owned company known for building large complex projects all over the country. And with the grandson of one of the company's founders heading up the new office, it was all but certain the branch would get all the necessary resources it needed to succeed.

As with all new "greenfield" operations, the sense of needing to land the first project in order to prove one's value to the construction community constantly wears on everyone at the office. And sometimes, no matter what you do in order to land that first project, it often times feels like an eternity before the first award comes.

Needing to get acquainted with the local subcontractor community, the new branch office was aware they couldn't put too many restrictions on who they allowed to bid their work. They knew that if they were going to be competitive against other more established general contractors in the Phoenix market, it was absolutely imperative they received help from the subcontractor community when it came to submitting the lowest possible bid at bid time.

One of those subcontractors willing to give the new general contractor in town the benefit of the doubt was the small electrical service contractor who had recently started his business venture as well. In a sense, both contractors needed one another in order for them to have the best chance for succeeding in the growing Phoenix market.

So with one successful project after another, not to mention a number of breakfasts, lunches and dinners with the grandson complements of the small electrical contractor, the small electrical contractor not only was able to forge a lasting relationship with the contractor for projects they were awarded in the future, but he was also able to forge a lasting relationship with the grandson and all of his executives and senior managers as well.

Fifteen years later, the small electrical service contractor became known as one of the larger preeminent electrical contractors in the state of Arizona.

In the story just told, the object of desire for the buyer, in this case the grandson of the founder was the need to make his mark running the new branch office for the large Midwest contractor. That emotion, through positive experiences, became directly tied to the small electrical service contractor who was willing to work with the grandson and his executives on a number of occasions to help make that desire a reality. In doing so, the grandson continued to remember over time who it was that helped him achieve that desired goal and rewarded the small electrical contractor with additional work. Said a bit differently, the buyer (grandson) reached a strong emotional attachment to the seller (small electrical service contractor), and in doing so, the buyer consistently maintained positive thoughts and/or emotions about the seller, resulting in the buyer only buying from the seller as opposed to someone else that the buyer had no attachment to.

If you will recall from a previous chapter in this book, I spoke about leadership's very important role in establishing an organizational culture, or belief if you will, that is conducive to long-term sustainability. A culture in part where business owners, executives and senior managers remain in constant communications with the entire organization, passionately promoting to everyone: a) "Why" it is the company is in business to begin with; b) "What" it is they believe in; c) the importance of operational alignment and synergy, i.e., a culture of interdependency; and d) customer and community development/involvement. In short, it's the very story of Apple and how the company, its products, its services, and its leader's legacy live on in the hearts and minds of its loyal customers for generations to come.

Some of you may have heard of Simon Sinek and *The Golden Circle*. If you haven't, I highly suggest you Google his TED presentation, "How Great Leaders Inspire Action."

As Mr. Sinek explains using *The Golden Circle*, the world as we know it is conditioned to communicate from the outside in when it comes to the "why," "how," and "what" a company does, i.e., its business purpose. Business's typically say or advertise first, "what" it is they do, followed by "how" they do it, and sometimes, "why" it is they do what they do.

If you look closely this is exactly how marketing is done, how sales are done, and basically, how all interpersonal communications are done. The "what" is clear and relatively easy for most employees and customers to articulate, but the "why" is not so clear, and not so easy for most to articulate. It is also why customer loyalty is so often hard to achieve.

When employees and customers can't reach an emotional attachment to the company, its products, services, and some cases its leaders, a reciprocal expression of goodwill or good faith can never occur in a sustainable environment. However, companies like Apple, who start with making sure their customers and employees understand the "why" first, subsequently working their way out to the "how" and "what" will always have an advantage over the competition due to an entrenched loyalty from its customer base.

Think about it from the perspective of what happens when you go to a social event where you'll be meeting strangers for the first time. What's the first question that you ask, or is asked of you?

Answer: "What is it that you do?"

If all a company wants to sell is "what" it does, customer loyalty can never be created. The reason for this is because we live in a society of multiple choices. Mr. Sinek explains, customer loyalty can only be created by those companies who emotionally and passionately speak directly to the part of a customer's brain that controls behavior; and that starts with "why" a company does what it does. If a company starts with "why" first, then works its way through "how" and "what," only then can customer loyalty have a chance to flourish.

In order to achieve customer loyalty, you have to remember, and follow, this one simple rule: The goal of any business purpose is not just to sell to customers who need or want what you have to offer. The goal is to sell to customers who believe what you as a company believe.

Time for a Mental Note

"People don't buy 'What' you do; they buy 'Why' you do it." (Simon Sinek)

This very same thought process by future business owners, executives, and entrepreneurs should also be applied to employees that get hired by a company. The goal of any company is not to hire people who need a job. The ultimate goal of a company is to hire people who believe what the company believes, and, because of this inherent synchronized belief structure, those same employees will also find a way to bring added value to the company through things like: (a) innovation and exploration; (b) a willingness to work hard and be productive; (c) a willingness to provide constructive feedback; and (d) community involvement.

Anyone can be a good or great employee, but most good and great employees never bring added value to a company without some sort of emotional attachment to the company. If a company hires people just because they think they will do a job, they will gladly work for the company's money and that's just about it. However, if companies hire people who believe what the company believes, they will gladly work for the company in a much more productive and meaningful way.

Loyalty begins as a person belief, a "value" if you will, and over time can become a very powerful force that bonds people and entities together. Loyalty truly is the Holy Grail of any business purpose.

11

Selling "Value" to Customers

For the past one hundred years or so the term "value" has not been absent from the lexicon of business owners, executives, and entrepreneurs. However, that is about to change in the coming decades as customers become more savvy consumers of goods and services aided by social media, digital platforms, and algorithms.

Today, sectors of the US economy who understand the power of technology know that selling "value" as opposed to price is not only more profitable, but it also helps create an inherent brand loyalty that conventional marketing techniques have failed to do in the past. Companies like Amazon have figured out that the majority of consumers no longer see the benefit of buying something cheap that doesn't last for an acceptable amount of time. Nor do consumers enjoy the inconveniences incurred by having to leave the comforts of their homes in order to go get something they need or want.

More and more, consumers today are embracing the concept of "You get what you pay for," and are therefore continuing to educate themselves on the actual "value-add" a product or service provides over the long run in lieu of buying on the cheap. At present, and more so in the future, business owners, executives, and entrepreneurs are developing digital platforms models and viral marketing schemes as a means to providing consumers with the knowledge they need in order to buy for "value."

But if you really want to know the true inside secret to selling, and selling "value" to customers beyond digital platform models and viral marketing schemes, all you have to do first is express a belief to customers in what it is you're doing, and the rest will come naturally. If customers believe that you believe in your product or service, it will give them the added confidence that they should believe in it too. Confidence being the key work here.

For business owners, executives, and entrepreneurs, consumer confidence is a very important and powerful metric to keep an eye on whether it's relative to a specific product, service, or entire economy as a whole. Would you buy a new car if you weren't 100 percent confident in the fact it was safe to drive?

Now I know what you're thinking, beyond keeping track of the number of units sold in a given period of time, or spending untold dollars generating marketing surveys mailed to customers who had previously purchased a product or service, how in the world would any business know how to effectively measure consumer confidence in a product or service in real-time even though someone may or may not have a purchased or service?

Answer: Digital platforms, viral marketing, and social media

Facebook, Twitter, Instagram, just to name a few, have the reach of millions of potential consumers at the touch of a finger. Want to know where to find a good and inexpensive sushi restaurant close to your current location, just ask anyone on a social media account, or if you happen to have access to an Apple iPhone simply look at the comments posted on the websites that Siri calls up for sushi restaurants near you. In today's world, for tech-savvy consumers, it's just that easy and convenient.

Here's what else business owners, executives, and entrepreneurs need to know and understand about consumer confidence, it separates the competition during both upturns and downturns in any economy. If consumer confidence is high about one particular product or service brand over another competing brand, guess which brand gets purchased more often than not? Here's an example of what I'm talking about and the power of mass social media at your fingertips.

Let's say for example you're in the market for a certain-sized flat-screen TV. You then ask two close friends who have similar size flat screen TVs if they like their particular brand, and both respond in a very positive manner. Since you have confidence in your friends not to lead you astray, you will probably go with the one that has a cheaper price. However, if they both happen to be priced almost the exact same, you then turn to social media to see what the masses have to say about the choice of both brands. After the results are in which brand do you think you will buy? The one with a handful of "thumbs up" or the one with thousands of "thumbs up."

See what I mean about the amount of confidence mass social media imparts on consumers in an accelerate timeframe?

I am convinced today, more so than ever, that business owners, executives, and entrepreneurs are truly missing out on sustainable wealth-building opportunities and benefits by not adopting a more advanced and technical way of managing and selling their products and services. One of the reasons for this is because business owners, executives, and entrepreneurs are still holding on tightly to the paradigm of chasing "Profitability" as the ultimate goal of business purpose; and in doing so, distracting the entire organization away from embracing a much broader "value-based"/"value-added" managerial culture.

"Value-based" management techniques assume that all operational decisions are based solely on personal and commercial values, while "value-added" analysis, assessment, and modeling are analytical methods that inherently isolate the marginal effectiveness (or contribution) that a performance metric provides to an operation over a comparative period of time. I know this may sound a bit new and confusing right now but it's really not as you will see.

Think about "value-based" management in terms of how a business goes about selling a product or service. Conventional wisdom tells most business owners, executives, and entrepreneurs that they should focus on selling their costs with a reasonable mark up. Why? Because it's easy and doesn't take a lot of creative effort. Not to mention, it's also a straight forward method for pricing, and, is pretty much the same way it's been done for generations.

If you've heard the answer once you've heard it one hundred times when a salesperson gets asked why the price of a particular product or service seems unreasonably high: "The price is the price," or "It is what it is, our costs plus a reasonable mark-up, take it or leave it." Attitudes that will never fly in the future by the way, trust me.

Look, anyone can sell their costs, especially if they openly show what those costs are to a customer. Getting a potential customer to *buy* what something actually costs presents no significant challenge to a seller because the buyer can see for him or herself they are not being taken advantage during the transaction. It's only when a seller tries to convince a customer to *pay* a higher price for the additional "value" being received that creates challenges for sellers. So why is that?

Time for a Mental Note

"Price is what you pay, Value is what you get."
(Warren Buffet)

Take for example the health of a company's revenue stream as one component of the operation whose quality of performance can directly impact a company's ability to achieve and maintain a required level of operational alignment, synergy, and liquidity. Instead of starting out with the conventional approach to pricing a product or service, let's look at how a business owner, executive, or entrepreneur should go about pricing his or her products or services from a "value-based" pricing perspective.

"Value-based" pricing, also referred to as "optimized pricing" is a pricing methodology or strategy that sets prices primarily on the value perceived by the customer rather than the actual cost of the product or service. Said a bit differently, "It's not what something costs it's what you can sell it for."

Time for a Mental Note

Not only does "value-based" pricing, or "optimized pricing," of a product or service increase the health of a company's revenue stream, it will also drive the company's marginal returns, i.e., profit, higher without negatively impacting the quantity of future sales.

In order for a business owner, executive, or entrepreneur to sell a higher price for their product or service, while simultaneously having the greatest impact on their bottom-line, it is imperative that the "value" received by the customer is recognizable and affordable. And the only way for a product or service to be affordable to the masses is if production costs continued to be controlled in such a way that the asking price being paid is at a mutually beneficial level to both the buyer and seller. An interdependency that encompasses operational efficiencies, consumer confidence, and the willingness to acknowledge that a benefit exists.

Organizations in the future, who strive to become dependent upon a culture of interdependency, where everyone is required to work together for a single purpose, will not only recognize higher levels of positive cash flow, but also too, find it much easier to sell "value" to potential customers more than willing to become brand loyalists. If you don't believe me, just spend some time researching the recent success stories of companies like Apple and the Boston Red Sox to name just a couple.

Time for a Mental Note

Sociotechnical refers to the interaction between a society's complex infrastructures, values, and behaviors and the technical aspects of a business's organization structure and processes. Sociotechnical is about "joint optimization" with a shared emphasis on achieving excellence in technical performance, and, the quality of work life for all employees. It's where systems are developed based on the relationships between social and technical elements that lead to the enhancement of productivity and personal well-being.

The first step in pricing 'Value' into a product or service is to understand how the fundamental components of "price," "cost," and "profit" actually relate to one another. "Price" being what a customer is willing to pay for a product or service, "cost" being the outlay of cash and/or credit incurred to produce a product or provide a service, and "profit" being the margin generated from the transaction.

In Western cultures such as the US, the mathematical relationship between "Price" (P), "Cost" (C), and "Profit" (B) is typically represented by the formula: $P = C + B$, where "Price" is a dependent result based on the amount of an arbitrary and anticipated value of "Profit" that is added to a value of anticipated "Cost" to produce a product or provide a service.

In non-Western or sociotechnical cultures like Asia, the mathematical relationship between "Price," "Cost," and "Profit is typically represented by the formula: $B = P - C$, where the desired "Profit" is the focal point of importance. "Price" is actually consider a fixed value based on extensive market research, for which the "Cost" of production is subtracted from.

Question, which of the two pricing methods prices in "value"? If your answer is the non-Western sociotechnical approach you would be correct, and here's why.

For over a century of industrialism "price" by Western standards has always been the result of adding a business's "cost" of production to an arbitrary value of "profit" business owners, executives, and entrepreneurs felt would be acceptable to the marketplace (trial by error if you will). If the product or service wouldn't sell in a timely manner the value of anticipated "profit" would be reduced; which in turn would lower the selling "price." A pricing process that eliminates any "value" to either the company or consumer, and one that would continue until an equilibrium point could be reached.

By non-Western or sociotechnical standards that have been around for about a half century, the amount of "profit" generated from a transaction has been determined to be a function of a predetermined "price" by which the "cost" of production is subtracted. Why? Because in non-Western or sociotechnical cultures "cost" of production is truly not a fixed value, but rather a variable with no limitations placed on how much "waste," i.e., movements of the hands and feet for starters, can be taken out of the deliverable process; and as a result, an inherent "value" gets created. A "value" that can be recognized by both the customer and company, and, one that is made affordable to the customer relative to the "price" that is paid for a product or service.

As the next generation of business owners, executives, and entrepreneurs move into the future they will not have the luxury of simply sitting behind a desk, pricing their products and services based solely on adding their "cost" to a desired level of "profit" if they ever expect to compete and succeed. Not only will business owners, executives, and entrepreneurs have to work hard at meeting the future demands of customers looking for the added "value" in the products and services they buy, but they will also have to work diligently at constantly creating "value" through operational alignment, synergy that achieves higher standards of performance, and the only way to do that is through continuous process improvement and "value-based" management.

"Value-based" management is defined as an approach to managing a business purpose focused on operational alignment that ensures the maximization of "value" delivered to both the company and its customers. It is an approach based on (a) creating "value," (b) measuring "value," (c) monitoring "value," and (d) delivering "value." It is also a managerial approach highly dependent upon a productive and positive interaction between everyone in the company, as well as, a positive interaction between the company and its customers.

Background: Baton Rouge, LA

In 2009, I was asked by the owner of a regional specialty contractor if I would be interested in managing a large hospital project located about seventy miles away from one of their branch offices.

Not sure at the time why a regional contractor with its size, capability, and reputation would be asking an outsider to oversee such a significant project, but I agreed to come on board with the company and handle the project.

The preconstruction services portion of the hospital project had actually started about a year or so prior to my arriving when the owner of the hospital and his construction manager preferred using one of the local electrical contractors, not the one I eventually went to work of. After a reasonably exhausting search, the owner and construction manager determined that they could not find an electrical contractor in the area who could provide the necessary expertise, manpower, or bonding capacity to meet the demands of the very large project. Then, roughly six months later, the owner/construction team finally decided to work with the large regional electrical contractor I went to work for because of their reputation for having expertise in healthcare work, and, the fact they could provide the necessary manpower and bonding for the project.

As part of the negotiations for being awarded the project, the electrical contractor agreed to perform design/assist services, along with installing the work under a T & M with Fee (that was less than 10 percent above all approved costs)—GMAX contract format.

Time for a Mental Note

A specialty contractor's fee of less than 10 percent is not uncommon for projects of this size and administered under a T & M-GMAX contract format. In fact, most of the larger specialty contractors operating today accept fees much lower than 10 percent as the size of the project gets larger in scope. Why? When the risks are much greater to the contactor, no one can say for certain other than to espouse the fact that if a contractor won't take a job at a lower fee, the owner will find a competitor that will.

Prior to my arriving to take over the project, the electrical contractor, along with the other MEP subcontractors, had spent months working with the owner, design team, and construction manager trying to hit an overall construction budget that had been established by the owner. Eventually, the time had come to start building the project; which also happened to be about the time I was brought in by the regional contractor's owner.

After reviewing the scope of work, associated pricing, and terms and conditions of the subcontract agreement, it occurred to me having a relatively strong working relationship with the construction manager that we had an opportunity to increase the health of our potential revenue stream, and eventual profit margin, well above the single digit previously agreed to before I arrived. With that in mind, I asked the regional contractor's branch manager if it would be acceptable for me to request a change in the contract format from a fee based GMAX to a more risky lump sum contract.

Looking at me somewhat perplexed, the branch manager asked me in response to my suggestion something along the lines of: "Why would we do that?" followed shortly behind by, "Why would they do that?" As to say we wouldn't get any better deal than the one we already had in place.

Time for a Mental Note

It should be noted that most contractors view a T & M with GMAX project as a relatively safe and low risk contract format; which it is so long as the GMAX portion of the contract is accurate. But here again, you have to remember that the acceptable pricing method by most contractors support the mathematical formula: $P = C + B$. Only this time, under a GMAX format, if the actual amount of "cost" comes in under the projected amount (which is what's expected using the sociotechnical pricing format), the "value" created by the contractor through his efficiencies and received by the customer will not be mutually beneficial to both the buyer and seller. Only the buyer will receive the benefit at the end of the day by paying a lower overall "cost" of the project. This is why contractors, at a minimum, need to consider negotiating a shared savings clause in all T & M with GMAX contracts.

Taking the necessary time to explain my reasoning, the branch manager started to pick up on some cost saving items that he felt could be recognized going forward. In fact, the branch manager, who was an extremely sharp individual with a lot of experience and who knew his way around contracts, recognized that most customers preferred not to work under the terms of a T & M based contract. Psychologically, and with some historical knowledge that supports their fears, customers typically prefer to fix their budgetary risk rather than leave it linger open-ended for an extended period of time.

Long story short, the branch manager and I collectively came up with a negotiating strategy that highlighted a number of benefits, i.e., "value-engineering," to the owner's electrical and communications design, along with benefits to the construction manager's overall budget. Our final selling point was that we were willing to take the risk of the design even though the construction documents weren't quite 100 percent complete at the time, and, provide a cost reduction of $160,000 to the overall electrical budget since we would no longer be required to internally track every cost relative to an audit by the owner/construction manager at the conclusion of the project. In the end, our negotiating strategy proved successful and the owner/construction manager team agreed to convert our contract to lump sum.

Fast forward about eighteen months when the project was commercially coming to a close and it was time for the branch manager and me to reconcile the anticipated profit margin generated from the project. As part of the process, the branch manager and I were called into a typical project review meeting with the branch manager's boss from corporate and the CFO.

At the meeting, and to both our surprise, what was originally assumed to be a typical postmortem review of a highly success major project quickly turned into an inquisition by both senior executives from corporate. An inquisition that inferred on a number of occasions that the branch manager and I were somehow hiding costs somewhere which allowed for a higher than normal profit to be recognized.

"Historically, we never see this kind of money being made on projects of this size," proclaimed the branch manager's boss.

But needless to say, this was not the branch manager's or my first rodeo. Between the two of us at the time, we had over sixty years of experience overseeing operations and projects, and not to sound arrogant, we knew how to make money from the opportunities that arose throughout the project's delivery. The excessively high profit margin was real.

As you just read in the story above, the benefits to such a managerial shift in order to find "value" can be staggering to say the least. So much so, that those within the same organization stuck in a conventional paradigm struggle to see any benefit, or value-add, even though the actual implementation of a "value-based"/"value-added" performance program was laid out right in front of them by two experienced employees. Benefits to both the company and customer that were recognized, not because the scope of work had changed, but because of a mind-set that emphasized a "value-based"/"value-added" performance program that was maintained from beginning to end.

Business owners, executives, and entrepreneurs of the future must come to grips with the fact that the upper limits of any benefit, i.e., return or "value," gained through a financial transaction, is not governed by some fictitious industry accepted standard, or by a morally acceptable amount of profit that seems reasonable for the amount of cost and risk being incurred. The very second business owners, executives, and entrepreneurs recognize this fact, i.e., paradigm shift, only then will they immediately comprehend the fact that the health of future revenue streams will now be in direct proportion to the benefits and "value" gained through "value-based"/"value-added" performance relative to the entire financial transaction.

Time for a Mental Note

*"If you want small changes in your life, work
on your attitude. But if you want big and primary
changes, work on your paradigm."* (Stephen Covey)

Now before you go off losing sleep thinking, "I can't start goug-
ing my customers," you need to give a little more thought to what I
just said about analyzing the upper limits of any benefit or "value" to
be gained through a financial transaction in the context of creating
and maintaining healthier revenue streams. If business owners, executives, and entrepreneurs truly want to increase the amount of profit
they generate over and above what their current industry paradigm
allows them to mentally accept, and/or recognize during reporting
periods, they first have to come to the realization that it's okay to
make more profit from the sale of a product or service than what
history has allowed in the past.

Take the construction industry for example where for years
construction managers and general contractors have been able to
secure work with an 8 percent to 10 percent fee on top of their costs
and allocated rate schedule. Likewise, if a specialty contractor could
secure work with margins in the 20 percent to 25 percent range on
top of their costs that work would be great to have as well. So why is
it that construction managers and/or general contractors consistently
settle these days for fees in the 2 percent to 4 percent range, while at
the same time specialty contractors are willing to settle for margins
on cost in the 7 percent to 10 percent range? And here's what's even
more abnormal about the contracting industry with all of its inherent financial and physical risks, when the size and complexity of the
work increases, contractors arbitrarily lower their fees and markups
thinking it makes them more viable and competitive, but yet, no
"value" gets added other than a lower price for the customer to pay.

Now if you were to tell me, or convince me, that the lower percentages of fees and markups were just for show on a bid proposal in
order to secure the work, I would rest a little easier; however, everyone in the construction industry knows that's not true.

Very few, if any, business owners, executives, or entrepreneurs operating today, especially in the contracting industry, in the US can actually generate substantially higher levels of return, including "value," via operational efficiencies. Why? Because finding "value" is not their focus, maximizing profit is.

Ask yourself this question: When you go to the bank for a loan, does the bank charge you a higher or lower interest rate on the principle if you increase your requested loan amount?

The obvious answer is you will be required to pay a higher interest rate. Why? Because logic tells the lender that the risk of not being paid back in full increases proportionally to the amount of money that is being loaned. Higher levels of exposure, i.e., risk, provides within itself the receiving of a higher level of benefit, i.e., "value," through the interest being paid for the risk being taken. As a result "value" to both the consumer, who is allowed to increase the amount of the loan, and the lender by receiving a higher interest rate on the amount of funds being loaned. Seems very reasonable, right?

As the next generation of business owners, executives, and entrepreneurs will begin to discover, "value" and "values" are two very different concepts that will weigh heavily on them when trying to meeting the future needs of customers. Why? Because "value-based"/"value-added" performance is much more than what something is worth to a buyer and seller.

What most people seek in the world today, and let's not forget that demographics, i.e., people, always precipitates economics, i.e., money and things, is the ability to maximize their own personal happiness, well-being, and satisfaction, not wealth. And because of this, we have learned that human desire dictates how money is used and spent, innately guided by a person's "value" system.

As we have also learned a person's "values" system controls their behavior over time, which includes guiding one's ability to know how money is to be used and spent. For example, have you ever wondered why a billionaire like Sam Walton, born before the Great Depression, continued to drive his 1979 Ford F150 pickup well into the twilight of his life?

Whether you are a student just learning about the commercial aspect of life, or a seasoned business owner, executive, or entrepreneur, it is absolutely essential to understand that if you want to be a commercial success in life, you have to have shared "values" with others, both internally and externally to the business purpose. If you don't believe me, read about Steve Jobs of Apple, Henry Ford of Ford Motor Company, along with other great visionaries of history. Why do I say this? Because once you tap into a consumer's "value" system, brand loyalty gets created.

- "I'll only buy Apple products."
- "I'll never drive anything but a Ford."
- "When comes to fast food we only eat at Chick-Fil-A."
- "You can have Walmart, we shop at Costco."
- "I'm a Country Western fan."

Sound familiar!

In order to truly grasp the genius of people like Steve Jobs, Henry Ford and other visionaries of the past, all one has to do is figure out a way to wrap one's own mind around the concept of trying to envision how the world is viewed by the majority of others based on time, place, and the shared "Value" system of the collective many. As complex and difficult as this may seem, it's really not if you block out all the background noise that life has to offer and really listen to what good, honest, hardworking people are needing, wanting, and saying regardless of what generation they were born in.

But what does all this have to do with businesses meeting the future needs of customers or being a "high performance" company?

Unlike the vast majority of businesses operating today who sell nothing except their "cost" plus an artificial amount of "Profit" for a product or service, progressive companies like Apple and Amazon sell much more than that. Progressive companies, like "high performance"–based companies, also sell their own company's cultural "value" system as well. A cultural "value" system that is not only progressive, "high performance" based, and understanding of an ever-changing world around them, but one that is steeped in an attitude of continuously improving a customer's experience as they continue to buy more and more products or services.

Take the record industry for example and how consumers listened to their favorite music. Up until 1964, consumers listened to their favorite music generated from vinyl records. From 1964, until the compact cassette became commercially viable in 1979 (remember the Sony Walkman), the magnetic tape cartridge called the "8-Track Tape" became the supplemental norm for consumers still listening to their music on record players. Then in 1982, technology shows up at the consumer's doorstep once again and delivers the compact disc (CD), taking the world by storm and virtually putting the vinyl record industry out of business. Then in 2001, Apple introduces the iPod that was able to store thousands of songs in a small handheld device.

Progressive companies understand that just because a means, method, procedure, or process worked well in the past, or in another area of the country or world, it doesn't necessarily mean that the same means, method, procedure, or process will be applicable or acceptable in another area, or, in the future for that matter. What future businesses owners, executives, and entrepreneurs have to remember is that consumers are constantly trying to seek out how best to maximize their own personal happiness, well-being, and satisfaction. Understanding this is simple concept about humans is the pathway to inspiring added "value" and creating brand loyalty.

Meeting the Demands of Future Customers through Operational Alignment, Synergy, and Liquidity

In business, there are two types of cultures, productive and nonproductive. Although both types of cultures abide by a hierarchical management structure, each have defining qualities that dramatically set them apart.

Productive cultures are operationally aligned in such a way that executives, managers, and supervisors are already aware of how decisions will ultimately be determined long before they're even announced to the rest of the organization. Nonproductive cultures, on the other hand, are at best dysfunctional, autocratic, and usually grope their way through daily activities constantly bumping into road blocks and stymied by diverging values and opinions.

Now ask yourself this question. Which of the two cultures do you see having the best chance of meeting the current and future demands of customers as the next generation of business owners, executives, and entrepreneurs either take over establish companies or emerge on the scene out of nowhere in the coming decades?

There is no arguing the fact that it is an absolute must for companies to generate net positive cash flow from one reporting period to the next; but in order to achieve and maintain a net positive cash flow in the digital age, new and well-established companies alike will have to view the consumers of tomorrow from the perspective of utilizing the speed and added convenience of emerging technologies. Technologies that continually improve a company's positive cash flow, and eventual levels of profitability, through operational alignment, synergy, and liquidity conducive to long-term growth and prosperity.

In order to accomplish this, new and well-established companies will be required to continually analyze data and project future consumer trends created by shifting demographics. A matching if you will between the future needs of consumers and how well the operational functions of a business are performing relative to projections made in the past. An absolute impossibility if an organization is not operationally aligned and capable of efficiently delivering a product or service.

Take Steve Jobs of Apple, or Bill Gates of Microsoft for example. Over the years Mr. Jobs has had to somehow align his company's operational capabilities in terms of efficiently producing compatible, yet integrated, hardware and software components that match the future needs and demands of customers. Similarly, Mr. Gates has had to align his company's operational capabilities to produce a homogeneous suite of software programs targeted to specific and unique customers. Today, both Apple and Microsoft have some of the highest cash reserves of any company, public or private, on the planet.

Yes, companies need to be profitable, as well as have the ability to continually drive top line revenue, in order to build up cash reserves. But driving down costs at the expense of both top line revenue generation and operational alignment is not the way to creating positive cash flow or meeting the future needs of customers. If you don't believe me, just take a look at what happen to Apple in 1996 and 1997 after the company had already parted ways with its visionary, Steve Jobs.

Background: Cupertino, CA

As most people know by watching all the movies and documentaries about the passing of one of Apple's founders, Steve Jobs, the company was founded around 1976. A year later, Jobs and his partners came out with the Apple II computer; then, seven short years later, Apple introduces the Macintosh.

For the next six years or so Apple became part of a revolutionary tidal wave of technological innovations. As the company grew and expanded its product lines, it became increasingly difficult for Jobs to focus on creating new products, sales, and the bottom line of the company. So much so that competitors continued to gnaw away at Apple's market share. Jobs had to make a choice. And the choice Jobs made was grounded in what he had a passion for, and that was innovation, marketing, and selling; leaving the management of the company up to an outsider named John Sculley in 1983.

Within two years of Sculley's hiring, the board of directors pushed Sculley to rein in Jobs and his urges to spend massive amounts of monies launching new and innovative products; which were mainly his ideas. Jobs resisted.

As the story goes, a power struggle ensued, and a short time later Apple's board of directors acted, eventually leading to Jobs resignation.

By 1996, after hiring and firing a number of CEOs for incalculable missteps relating to product line development, marketing, and a weakened stock price, faced with a seemingly unrecognizable future, Apple's board of directors eventually gave one of their board members the CEO's chair to try and right the ship once and for all.

The new CEO, who had made a name for himself as a turnaround artist during his time as CEO of National Semiconductor, immediately started making changes that focused primarily on keeping costs below the sales revenue. His reasoning for making such changes in a short amount of time was voluminous; sighting a shortage of available cash, poor product quality, and an undisciplined corporate culture. In other words, the new CEO felt that focusing on internal concerns would eventually lead to Apple's eventual survival and viability.

In an attempt to correct these deficiencies, the new CEO conducted massive layoffs and cut whatever costs he felt would make the most impact in the shortest amount of time. Unfortunately, time was not on the new CEO's side as the company's stock price continued to plummet along with its market share.

Out of options, and on the brink of becoming extinct, to the new CEO's credit, he convinced the board of directors in 1997 to purchase the company Jobs started after leaving Apple. It was called NeXT. The deal for NeXT would also see the return of Jobs as an advisor.

Then, not long after Jobs's returned, a twist of fate happened to the new CEO. Apple's board of directors removed the new CEO and made Jobs the company's interim CEO and immediately took the opposite approach of the outgoing CEO and started restructuring the company's product lines in an attempt to broaden the company's reach to perspective customers; which in turn, would start generating revenues again. And as we all know, the rest as they say is history!

Companies today, not to mention the investment community on Wall Street, have paid very close attention to what can happen to a company's level of profitability if top line revenues are not consistently forecasted to reach certain levels over time. As in the story of Apple, all the cost cutting in the world, and the operational misalignment that accompanies it, cannot sustain an adequate of level of positive cash flow for any extended period of time without top line revenues being generated.

In other words, the only way a company today, and in the future for that matter, can remain viable and sustainable is if it can consistently generate a positive cash flow through both top line revenue creation, and, optimizing its operational alignment by matching its ability to deliver a product or service with that of current and future demands of customers.

Here are three prime examples of what I'm talking about: Amazon, Twitter, and Uber.

As you most of you know, Amazon, Twitter, and Uber have become successful even though they have consistently fell short of generating a reported profit for any extended period of time. So how can this be you may ask?

Answer: By one of the following three ways:

a) Purposeful Reinvestment: Amazon exemplifies this approach by choosing to reinvest most, if not all, of what it makes back into the business as a means to fueling top line growth. Amazon has continued this approach for over twenty years, content to focus on growth in lieu of profits.

b) Hopeful Expansion: Twitter falls into this approach. Propelled by an acquisition model, Twitter's intent is to reach some level of profitably that is sustainable in the near future, however, in order to accomplish this feat, actual expenses of the consolidated conglomerate eventually has to start dropping precipitously, and disproportionately more, in relation to its actual revenue growth.

c) Initial Growth: Companies like Uber start out showing incredible growth potential, which attracts investors who accept the fact that, initially, profits will be lagging behind for some period of time. As along as confidence in the company's future revenue growth models remain high, investors will be temporarily content for the time being, however, they will eventually expect profits to be generated at some point.

I can't tell you how many times in the past I've heard a business owner, i.e., contractor, tell me something along the lines of: "If I can't make a profit on a job, I don't want to do it," as if they're somehow clairvoyant about the outcome of a project or business venture before they're even awarded a contract.

Every time I hear this supercilious comment coming from a business owner, I think to myself as I shake my head in disbelief, how in the world could they possibly know if they're going to make a profit on a project before it even gets started given all the things that can and do go wrong throughout a process; especially in construction?

The reality is, they don't.

It is virtually impossible for any business owner to know, or predict, if they will ever make one dollar of profit on any project or venture. The unvarnished truth of the matter is every business owner who has ever been awarded a contract to provide a product or service has lost money through latent operational inefficiencies, many of which they never knew existed, and to this day still don't.

What the business models of Amazon, Twitter, and Uber have taught us about providing a product or service in the digital age is the simple fact that even though profit margins might be razor thin at times, an operation's ability to cash flow and pay for current and future obligations is the bedrock for survival. And the only way this happens is if the operation itself has the means to stay aligned and liquid, which doesn't mean it has to be profitable all the time.

The fact of the matter is, when a business's liquidity is at stake, no amount of calculable profit being generated and recorded from one reporting period to the next has any tangible value to a business survival in real-time. Again, you have to keep in mind that profit is a value dependent upon two variables at any given time, i.e., revenues and costs, and therefore, its value continues to change relative to the ebb and flow of business activities and operational performance. Apple found this out the hard way in 1996 and 1997 if you remember.

Step back for a second and really think about what I'm trying to convey here because it goes directly to the heart of this book. In essence, if a business cannot pay its bills, which includes paying its employees for their time, service, and effort in a timely manner, it cannot survive. Profit, generated by a mathematical formula and reflected on a financial statement from one month to the next has absolutely no value and no buying power in real-time, but cash-on-hand (or the availability to cash) does.

Time for a Mental Note

Look at this from a personal perspective. You and your family are getting hungry so you need to go out and buy some groceries. In the meantime, a bitter cold front just moved into the area and it's important to keep everyone warm, not to mention the house so pipes don't freeze. As you go out to the store to get the groceries, you stop by the mailbox and in it you find a letter from the utility company informing you that since your last month's payment is delinquent, they will be shutting off your electrical service in three days' time if you don't bring your account current. Also in the mailbox was another letter that contained your bank statement. Knowing you have hungry mouths to feed and a utility company about to turn off your power to the house, you quickly open up the statement to see what your available fund's balance happened to be at the closing date of the statement. What you discover is, there is nowhere near enough available funds in your bank account until the next pay day to buy the necessary groceries, and, bring the utility company account current.

As most know, it is very unlikely that either the grocer or utility company would take a check stub from the week before showing how much your take home pay is as collateral for payment. The same thing happens in business when companies are no longer able to pay their bills either. Showing employees and creditors a profitable financial statement as collateral for past due payments of wages benefits, or bills is an unlikely approach to having anyone extend the company more credit for goods and services.

If you look closer at Amazon, Twitter, and Uber, they are all buoyed by either reoccurring organic cash flow, investment capital coming into their businesses, or an ability to borrow cash, all of which going toward paying for current and future obligations, which directly affects their operational sustainability. What this also means is that so long as customer satisfaction remains intact, cash flow can be sustained and obligations (short-term and long-term) can be addressed in a timely manner. Which means in the end, consistently showing a profit is really not the top priority when compared to meeting the future demands of customers and hitting "internal," not "external," operational performance metrics.

Time for a Mental Note

In an article written by Jessica Stillman for *Inc.* magazine, Ms. Stillman points out a very interesting position held by Jeff Bezos, CEO of Amazon, when it comes to competitors focusing more on generating margins, i.e., profits, then any other aspect of their business. In part, Ms. Stillman writes:

> *"Recently on his blog current Microsoft employee and former private equity fund partner Tren Griffin suggested you go straight to the source, helpfully combing through Bezos' public utterances for valuable nuggets of wisdom.*
>
> *Inc.com reached out to ask if we could round up a few of the quotes he unearthed. Here's a sampling:*
>
> "Your margin is my opportunity."
>
> *As Griffin explains "Bezos sees a competitor's love of margins and other financial 'ratios' as an opportunity for Amazon since the competitor will cling to them while he focuses on absolute dollar free cash flow and slices through them like a hot knife through butter."*
>
> *"Bezos spelled out his focus on absolute dollar free cash flow in his 2004 letter to shareholders. He is not about to run his company based on a ratio much beloved by someone outside the company, such as a Wall Street analyst," Griffin elaborates. Are you looking focused on the right numbers for your business or are you more worried about hitting metrics that someone else told you matter?"*

So the question becomes, how do companies of today and tomorrow become more like Amazon, Twitter, and Uber, as the future of the US economy unfolds, particularly starting in 2030?

Answer: Companies of today and tomorrow must strive to meet the standards established for "high performance" companies where all that matters is positive cash flow through the creation of top line revenues and an operational alignment that matches a company's ability to deliver a product or service with the needs of its customers.

In their own unique way, owners and executives of "high performance" companies embrace the concept of operational alignment by continually focusing everyone's attention on three undeniable requirements for staying in business: (a) customer satisfaction, (b) creating positive cash flow, and (c) embracing the benefits of lean production. At the same time, owners and executives of "high performance" companies are constantly on the lookout for policies and procedures that inadvertently impact a positive customer experience, deter operational progress, or stymie individual creativity.

"High performance" companies absolutely do not gravitate toward formulating and publishing a lot of rules, regulations, policies, and procedures in order for their organizations to efficiently and effectively deliver products and/or services to customers at the highest level. "High performance" companies understand all too well that when the number of rules, regulations, policies, and procedures increase, trust in judgement, along with the morale of their managers and supervisors, decrease precipitously; not to mention the stifling of everyone's creativity.

"High performance" companies also know that if their organization is operationally aligned there should never be any reason for a prolonged internal conflict as to how best to proceed with a process or decision. To "high performance" companies, everyone should know the values, beliefs, goals, and purpose of the company, and any deviation from those values, beliefs, goals, or purpose of the company without extenuating circumstances is never tolerated. In other words, the values, beliefs, goals, and purpose of the company automatically becomes the ultimate decision maker whenever an internal dispute or conflict arises; but more importantly, they inherently become the ultimate guideposts for any decision regardless if a dispute or conflict arises or not.

"High performance" companies believe to their core that what it is they do as an organization is never enough to meet the future demands of customers. In other words, the light at the end of a tunnel for "high performance" companies is truly not viewed as the end of a journey but rather the cornerstone for a new beginning to be built upon; just like Apple, under the leadership of Steve Jobs and Steve Wosniak, who didn't stop after their successful launch of the Apple II in the late 1970s and early 1980s.

Background: Leavenworth, KS

In 1988, I joined a medium sized electrical contractor as a project manager assigned to one of the major automotive plants in the area. At the time, the medium sized contractor had annual revenues in the mid-$20 million range, with a goal set by its owner to be the largest electrical contractor in the area.

Prior to joining the medium-sized electrical contractor, I had to have a face-to-face interview with its owner; and because I was working for another contractor in Phoenix at the time on a large project that was starting to wrap up, between the owner's schedule and mine there was not a whole lot of time to get together. So the owner asked me if I would be interested in coming to his office over the Fourth of July weekend. He suggested that I travel to the area on that Friday, and we could meet the next day, Saturday. Right away, I knew this owner was special because he was more than willing to give up his Saturday over the Fourth of July weekend just to meet with me.

At the meeting, the owner laid out his vision for the company, which I didn't think much about it at the time because in my narrow view of things I was there to interview for a project manager's position. But a few years later, it finally dawned on me one day looking back at that interview how impressive it was for someone to know exactly where he was about to take a journey having never been down that particular path before. And as I look upon that time today, it's even more impressive to see that the owner actually did what he set out to do, and that was to become the largest, most profitable, company in the area.

To better understand the extraordinary feat this owner accomplished, you have to first realize where the medium sized electrical contractor was started from thirty years prior.

Started in 1957 by his parents, the medium sized electrical contractor had only one office at the time located in Leavenworth, KS, with a population of less than forty thousand, and an hour's drive from Kansas City. But to the owner, however, the key to his entire growth plan was to get established in the Kansas City market sooner rather than later.

By the time I arrived in late summer 1988, every office in the main building was filled, as was a supplemental office trailer set up in an adjacent lot. And although the owner had just recently bought a small electrical contractor in Kansas City that could accommodate some of the overflow of employees, he knew he had to find a much larger facility to support his growth and relocation plans; which actually did occur a couple years later.

During this same period of time, the owner was becoming more and more active in the electrical industry's very large and influential trade association, NECA (National Electrical Contractors Association). So much so, that in 1991, in the midst of all of his growth and expansion plans, the owner ran for, and was elected to, their highest office, national president.

What is important to note at this juncture is that the medium-sized electrical contractor was classified as a "union" contractor working under a collective bargaining agreement, and over the previous twenty-five years or so, "union" work throughout the country had been in a decline.

Knowing this at the time, even in the midst of implementing his own growth strategy, the owner still maintained his loyalty to being a "union" contractor. And because of his commitment to the "union" industry, the owner ran his campaign for national president on a platform to do whatever he could to slow the rate of decline of "union" work being awarded to member contractors. Also too, it was the owner's desire to help other member contractors get the operational tools they needed to compete in their respective markets against both "union" and "nonunion" competitors. Tools that would allow for (a) better cooperation between member contractors and their local unions, (b) improving morale and productivity of the workplace, and (c) better educating their future managers and field supervisors to meet the future demands of the industry. The owner eventually won the election and was now faced with the daunting task of having to deliver the promises he made on the campaign trail.

For me, while all this was going on with the owner, I had been spending most of my time based at multiple jobsite offices throughout the area in lieu of an office at the main headquarters, which by this time had moved from Leavenworth to Kansas City. And although I was remote from the main office, the owner continued to maintained contact with all of his onsite managers, even though he had group VPs with similar responsibilities. He was definitely an owner who wanted to stay engaged with the comings and goings of his company as much as possible.

Then one day I received a call from the owner. He asked if I knew anything about Total Quality Management (TQM). I immediately said "No!" In typical fashion, the owner told me not to worry about it because I would soon enough. Before closing out the call, the owner also told me that I needed to be at a joint IBEW/NECA meeting in two days, and said he would explain later what it was going to be all about.

Now you have to understand a couple of things here. This was 1992, and the Kansas City economy was still dealing with the after effects of the 1990–1991 recession, which meant, there had not been a lot of work going in the area for quite some time. So little work in fact that it got to a point where both the NECA contractors and local IBEW union seemed to be openly blaming the other for so many electricians being out of work.

The second thing you have to realize here is that the IBEW (International Brotherhood of Electrical Workers) had also been internally training their business managers and business agents to be on the lookout for contractor sponsored programs that would take work away from their members, and Total Quality Management (TQM) programs were very close to the top of their list.

The day of the meeting came, held at the chapter office of NECA. In attendance for the IBEW were their Business Manager and a number of other union officials. NECA was represented by the owner as their national president, NECA's local Chapter Manager and his assistant, my direct report at the company and me. As with most gatherings when the opposing parties to a collective bargaining agreement are in the same room, conversations amongst participants are generally polite, but very guarded; and this meeting was no different.

To open the meeting, the IBEW's Business Manager holds up a booklet entitled, *Employee Participation Programs—In a Labor/ Management Environment, A Statement of Policy and Guidelines for IBEW Local Unions,* and proclaiming to everyone in attendance that he had just sat through 9 hours of training on how to combat contractor initiated productivity enhancement programs. But to his credit, he did go on to say that he would keep an open mind to what was being proposed by NECA and the owner of my company. Luckily for the owner and his highly anticipated TQM program, the business manager was actually a very sharp individual who recognized the need for things to change in the marketplace or more of his members would be out of work.

After about an hour of back and forth, the owner and the IBEW Business Manager agreed that the owner would offer up a major project as a test case before any broader productivity enhancement program would be discussed or implemented. And above all else, the program could not have any reference to "management" in the title.

Shockingly, the test case project agreed to by the owner and IBEW Business Manager was a new, very large high school being built by a non-union general contractor which had just been awarded to my company. I say shockingly, because as most specialty contractors in the construction industry will attest to, whether during good times or bad, school work is not the easiest type of work to make any money on, especially when you are a "union" contractor competing against numerous other non-union competitors. But the genius of the owner, he knew that if he was going to make his mark on the industry, he couldn't be viewed as sandbagging his own initiative, even if it was the early 1990s and economic times being what they were.

Between the owner's growth initiative for the company, and now this potentially ground-breaking initiative that could impact the entire construction industry, there was much more that could go wrong than could go right in the weeks and months to come. And if the economic times and razor thin margin type of work to be performed wasn't bad enough, the owner had to also agree to a number of stipulation by the local union's Business Manager before he would agree to participate in the program. Stipulations like:

a) As part of the negotiations for agreeing to participate, the business manager stipulated that this had to be advertised as a joint project between the IBEW and NECA, and not a management (NECA) led initiative. This also meant the word "management" could not be used unless the word "labor" was attached to the title as well.

b) The IBEW would appoint a "union" steward starting day one to insure that both the collective bargaining agreement and guidelines for the initiative were adhered to by the NECA contractor. The owner and NECA's Chapter Manager agreed so long as the steward was a working steward and had not been terminated by the company in the past for cause.

c) The IBEW Business Manager would select one of its "E-Board" members to work on the project (E-Board refers to an executive committee member). The owner and NECA Chapter Manager agreed so long as the "E-Board" member had not been previously terminated for cause by the company.

d) The IBEW Business Manager wanted to insure that the ratio of fifty-five-year-old members stipulated in the collective bargaining agreement would be adhered to on the project at all times. The ratio at the time was every fifth employee assigned to the project had to be fifty-five years or older.

e) The IBEW Business Manager insisted that at least one female member, at a minimum, would be employed at point during the project, and definitely not at the end.

f) The IBEW Business Manager stipulated that no "union" member could be called out by name unless it fell within the guidelines of the collective bargaining agreement.

g) The owner and NECA Chapter Manager stipulated that an industry consultant trained in Total Quality Management (TQM) would be assigned to the program to assist in the implementation and assessment of the initiative, which included developing the appropriate benchmarks to be measured. The IBEW Business Manager would only agree to this so long as no member would be terminated for not meeting any established labor unit standard of installation. Subsequently, this stipulation by the owner and NECA Chapter Manager created a lot of discussion, which ultimately led to the forming of a disputes resolution committee made up of equal members of NECA, the IBEW, and the owner's management staff.

Although, I was working under other senior executives at the company overseeing projects in three states, Missouri, Kansas, and Colorado, the owner made it clear to them all that I was to be provided the necessary time and support for whatever training I needed to make his signature Total Quality program a success. Training that actually took me all the way to Gifu, Japan, to learn the inner workings of the Toyota Production System under the Shingujitsu Group.

Three years later, after hugely successful results were advertised, the owner's TQ program, along with members of the team who helped build the high school project, was the featured article in the December 1995 edition of NECA's national publication, *Electrical Contractor*. And if you were also wondering how the IBEW Business Manager felt about the program once all the results were in? He issued this statement in the local IBEW quarterly newsletter: "*I am convinced that the success or failure in regaining our market share will, in part, be determined by those with the business acumen and ability to work smarter-not harder, at every level of the employer organization."*

But here's what is most interesting about the initiative. It didn't take the owner and his executives three years to start implementing all the positive things that came out of the test case. In fact, within two years after the high school project got underway, and early results started to become verifiable and substantiated, the company's board of directors officially proclaimed that the entire company would adopt the TQ initiative and immediately begin training all of its existing and new employees in the techniques of total quality.

At this point, I'm going to fast forward to 1996, when the company in this story started knocking on the $100 million revenue door. If you want to know why a stipulated profit amount or profit percentage recorded from one reporting period to the next has no true tangible bearing on a company's short-term "liquidity" or long-term "sustainability," look no farther than this company's attributes:

a) As with all great leaders, the owner set the vision for the future and attitude of the culture, constantly communicating with his senior executives in order to insure the company stayed on track. It was text book operational alignment at its finest even before the TQ initiative was implemented.

b) The owner surrounded himself with competent and loyal senior executives who didn't necessarily agree with one another all the time, but eventually would find common ground and ultimately add a collaborative value to the company. It's what synergy is all about (1 + 1 > 2).

c) Being NECA's national president for roughly four years, and managing two offices, the owner found himself having to be away from at least one the offices for days at a time; and because of his short-term absence, the owner needed senior executives he could trust to oversee the day to day operations and implement any new initiatives or processes that came out of the company's continuous process improvement environment. By being a "servant leader," the owner was able to multi-task a number of operational assignments both within and out of the company.

d) The owner and his executives quickly picked up on something roughly nine months into the Total Quality (TQ) initiative at the high school project that helped provide an increased confidence level that the track the company was on was the right one. It was the concept of "benchmarking"; which became the primary staple of the TQ initiative. Surprisingly, what "benchmarking" uncovered was a number of excessive labor units, along with a number of unachievable ones, being employed during the company's estimating process. After insuring there wasn't an anomaly with just a handful of labor units being measured and reported on the test project, the owner and his executives embarked on an ambitious program to continually scrub their entire estimating data base as each new project in the pipeline implemented "benchmarking" for compliance. The philosophy of: "If you can't measure it, you can't manage it" became the new mantra for both office and field personnel to adopt.

Time for a Mental Note

Most construction trade associations publish established labor units for the specific types of installation contractors encounter on projects. For the electrical industry, most, if not all, contractors use the NECA Manual of Labor Units (XYZ) Edition. Knowing this, provides a competitive advantage to those contractors who consistently benchmark their production, while at the same time, creates a competitive disadvantage to those contractors who don't benchmark.

e) As "benchmarking" took hold, the company started to measure everything that involved the movement of hands and feet. From the cost of writing a purchase order to how long it took to drill a single hole in concrete and set an anchor. There was nothing considered off limits when it came to measuring how long it took to install something.

f) As a means to further enhance the company's ability to be more productive by continuously improving processes, both in the office and field, the owner and his executives started to look at different types of tools and equipment that supported their standard types of installation. This is also where the owner and his executives found huge areas for improvement. For example, when they analyzed their cable/wire pulling equipment, they found that their equipment manager was continually buying the same make and model tugger to pull the cable/wire, which had a fully loaded pulling speed of around six feet/minute. Not only did they educate themselves on the different makes and models of cable/wire pulling equipment with higher load to pulling speed ratios, but they also educated their field supervisors on how to request the right pulling equipment for the application it was going to be used for. It was no wonder the company was finding increases to its operational efficiencies to the tune of 25 percent, if not more, in areas.

g) To further enhance the productivity of the company, the owner and his executives felt it was extremely important to embraced individual creativity and innovation, solely geared toward improving processes by any member of the company. On a quarterly basis, a continuous process improvement committee would convene to review improvement initiatives and pick the most innovative idea for process improvement by one office staff member and one field person. Winners would receive a very handsome gift, which didn't take long for word to get out as to what it was, and in the end, ultimately enticing everyone in the company to become part of continuous process improvement program.

h) Armed with this new found confidence in the estimating data base, combined with an advancing culture of innovation and continuous process improvement, the owner knew there was a latent competitive advantage he could gain in the marketplace when bidding future projects since the majority of competitors, "union" and non-union, throughout the country typically used the same industry standard labor units as a basis for their estimates. And because of this industry mind-set, the owner immediately started to have his executives hold monthly *"benchmarking"* review sessions with various project managers and field supervisors handling certain types of projects. In turn, the executives would take the data from the review sessions and use it with the estimating staff on future bids—honing estimated labor units up and down to levels they felt reasonably sure the available field crews could meet on a regular basis. Not only did these monthly review sessions continue to operationally align processes, but they also created an undeniable synergy between members of the project management staff, estimating department, and field supervisors who historically are at odds with one another when projects start to go bad and folks start looking for others to blame.

i) As time marched on, and the economy started to rebound, the frequency of larger projects in the area started to increase. It was also a time in construction when the industry started to witness a change in how large projects were being delivered to certain customers in a given marketplace—it was the advent of "construction management." As construction managers gradually started to replace traditional general contractors, open participation from the subcontractor community became a way of life when it came time to provide bid and/or cost proposals for future work.

j) With each new project to be delivered under a construction management agreement, subcontractors were now being asked to expose their proposed mark ups and fees on T

190

& M—GMAX cost proposals as opposed to just providing aggregate pricing breakdowns for specific scopes of work. Once word eventually started leaking out, post-award, as to what the successful competitors were showing on their bid forms for mark ups and fees, it didn't take long before the subcontractor community reacted by tightening up their margins in the hopes of being selected on future projects. An act that did nothing more than drive down prices for construction work, while simultaneously driving up the frequency of contractor disputes.

k) Interestingly enough, none of these new nuances for procuring and delivering work by construction managers deterred the owner and his executives from moving forward with the vision for the company. The owner and his executives knew they had a distinct advantage over their competition with their new process improvement program, and they weren't afraid to use it when necessary.

l) During the time when specialty contractors didn't have to expose their mark-ups and fees to general contractors, electrical contractors were regularly seeing work being procured with 15 percent to 18 percent markups added to their cost structure. Now that the subcontractor community is being asked to show their proposed mark-ups and fees, electrical contractors were starting to see a decay in their level of markups and fees being awarded relating to various projects. As word continued to leak out with each subsequent project in terms of who was being awarded the project, along with their competitive mark-ups and fees, it seemed as though the subcontractor community was content to continue lowering their requested amounts with each subsequent bid. And in this one particular market, the one electrical contractor who seemed to consistently be awarded most of the work was the contractor I was working for at the time. So much so, that competitors could be overheard discussing at industry functions that if the company I was with continued to bid jobs as low as we were, it wouldn't be long before we would be out of business.

m) What our competitors didn't know, is that our owner and his executives knew exactly what they were doing. Armed with the knowledge that the competitors in the market were more than likely using the industry standard labor units, possibly discounted by some level, it really didn't matter to the owner and executives what amount of percentage mark-up or fee they needed to show on a proposal to secure the work because they had a pretty fair idea just about how much they were going make, profit-wise, through operational efficiencies given their historical installation data.

It's important to note that in order to provide customers with the greatest amount convenience and 'Value' for a product or service there is no requirement what so ever for an organization to embrace a specific quality initiative, set of performance standards, or digital platform model. In fact, the only ingredient necessary for a "high performance" company to reach the highest level of performance is their ability to embrace whatever technology and operational standard of excellence that is conducive to their cultural needs, which in the end, will ultimately drive customer satisfaction.

To survive in any business endeavor, generating a profit is important, however, as we've have just learned, in order for a company to generate a profit other elements of the business venture have to be aligned with the needs of customers or the business ventures turns out to be all for not. For business owners, executives, and entrepreneurs searching for a pathway to success in the coming decades they must find a way to cultivate a cultural environment that inherently focuses every employee's attention on the need to achieve and maintain a level of operational alignment, synergy, and liquidity that meets the short-term and long-term obligations of the company. A cultural environment that embraces change through its constant pursuit and achievement of higher levels of customer satisfaction.

Creating Healthy Revenue
Streams over Time

As we have already read in previous chapters, top line numbers are typically generated through conventional pricing means. Businesses can also increase their top line numbers by acquiring other companies, or, branching off with complementary offices in different markets. Whatever the case, revenue generation is the core operational aspect of any business purpose.

When it comes to generating top line numbers for a business, operational rank and file employees working throughout the organization, unless they're apart of the executive management group or accounting department where the term "revenue" is used on a regular basis, usually converse amongst themselves in terms of "sales" or "billings," and never in terms of revenue recognition. This is unfortunate, because it truly shows a lack of awareness by front line managers and supervisors whose sole purpose in having that position is to control the bottom line, and by extension, insuring that a business's revenue stream constantly stays healthy over time.

Time and again, you will read in this book how operating a business is about so many other things than just generating a profit. If business owners, executives, and entrepreneurs would just simply focus on the primary concepts of (a) customer loyalty; (b) operational alignment, synergy, and liquidity; (c) cash flow; and (d) creating healthy revenue streams, the least of their worries would be about generating a profit.

Time for a Mental Note

The term "profit" in construction can be defined as the beneficial amount gained over and above each dollar of revenue that is recognized through a contractor's billing process to customers. The amount of "profit," after the last dollar of revenue has been received from a customer, indicates to a contractor how efficient, or inefficient, the operation functioned in delivering the project to the customer on behalf of the company.

So what exactly are healthy revenues and revenue recognition all about?

To answer this question, we need to start by understanding what revenues are and how they eventually become recognized by businesses from an accounting point of view.

In an effort not to take too deep of a dive into accounting and financial terms, it's important to know that the accounting world we all live in in the US is governed by a set of standards, principles, and rules entitled GAAP (Generally Accepted Accounting Principles). These are guidelines used by most CPAs for both personal and business tax returns.

When it comes to "revenue recognition" for businesses, GAAP has two basic rules that need to be adhered to:

a) The revenue generated from the sale of goods or services are to be recorded in the company's financial statements when the seller has transferred to the buyer all reasonably tangible risk and rewards of ownership, and, when the amount of the exchange or consideration, i.e., selling price, can be reasonably identified or determined.

b) The revenue generated from the sale of goods or services are to be recorded when the collection is reasonably assured.

In a nutshell, GAAP is saying that there has to be first a value placed on the exchange in order for it to be recorded on a business's books; and secondly, before the recording can take place, there has to be a reasonable assurance by the recording entity that the corresponding value of whatever the medium of exchange is, usually cash, that the full value of the exchange will actually take place. If there is no assurance that the exchange or consideration will ever take place, then the entity doing the recording is not allowed by GAAP to recognize the value of the exchange or consideration as revenue. By GAAP standards, timing is an important component of when revenues can be recognized.

When applying GAAP standards to most industries, you have to be aware that a number of contracts and/or purchase agreements typically extend well beyond a 30 day period or cycle. With that being the case, GAAP standards allow for two acceptable accounting methods that businesses can use for revenue recognition: (a) percent complete or (b) completed contract.

Now, before I go any farther, I want to intentionally digress for a second here because this is absolutely critical to the health of a business's revenue stream, along with its ability to achieve and maintain a required level of operational alignment, synergy, and liquidity in real time. It begins with a certain attitude cultivated from top management before it permeates its way throughout the entire organization.

I use the term "attitude" because I have been amazed over the years watching business owners, executives, and entrepreneurs of both large and small companies struggle with their cash flow needs. It's no wonder that the number one reason for business failures is due to poor cash flow management. But even armed with this knowledge of history the majority of business owners, executives, and entrepreneurs operating today still do not make cash flow management their number two priority, just behind developing customer "loyalty." Why is this?

Answer: Again, it's attitude.

Time and again, I've heard business owners, executives, and entrepreneurs say something similar to the effect: "I don't want my managers and supervisors worried about billing and collecting money, I have an accounting department (or clerk as the case may be) responsible for that. I want my managers and supervisors focused generating profit." And you know what, these are the same business owners, executives, and entrepreneurs who: (a) continually go to the bank needing a short-term infusion of cash; (b) hold payments from subcontractors and venders that support their operations; (c) worry that they won't be able to cash flow a future contract or purchase agreement they really want; and (d) make up the vast majority of companies that fail because of poor cash flow management.

In the end, managing a business's cash flow is all about attitude. If business owners, executives, and entrepreneurs don't make it a priority for those closest to it, then, there is no reason to believe that those closest to it would ever be worried about it.

Background: Phoenix, AZ

Remember the story I told in an earlier chapter about the contractor who wanted to hire me, but couldn't find the time to interview me because he was too busy building his new luxury home at the base of a mountain?

Within days after starting at the company, I was introduced to a number of folks internal and external to the company, but very few seemed to be venders calling on the contractor, which is a recognizable practice for most specialty contractors. Not only did this strike me as odd, because one of the reasons I was hired was to procure work for the company and if you don't have vender support for pricing, you will typically not be competitive when you submit your bid, but I also couldn't figure out at the time what was really going on.

Time for a Mental Note

Venders are obviously a key component of a specialty contractors operation before, during, and after the award of a construction contract. Before a contract is awarded, venders help the estimating department with pricing quotes. During a construction project, venders support the entire supply chain management of the deliverables. After a project has been completed, venders provide close out documents and contractual warranties for materials and services they supplied to the project.

A few weeks had passed since my initial hiring and I was asked to manage a relatively small project while continuing to bid new work that was coming on the market. Needing both material to purchase for the existing project, and pricing quotes for future estimates, I was in desperate need of a vender or two who could help me fulfill my job functions. Asking one of the other project managers who I should call, I was given the name of his primary vender. I then called the vender and set up a time to go meet about my needs. Here again, this was unusual because venders would typically make the effort to call on contractors at their offices, not the other way around.

As I arrived at the vender's fairly large facility, I could see the operation was set up like most distributors who serviced the electrical contracting industry. They had their typical long counter up front for off the street sales and pickups, and sales offices located directly behind the counter. The only one difference from my seldom visits to other vender's facilities was that this time the sale's rep I was supposed to meet with didn't invite me back to his office. He only wanted to discuss my needs over the counter, and at that very moment, I knew something was off about this whole thing. That is, until he told me the rest of the story.

As it turns out, the contractor who was so busy building his new luxury home at the base of a mountain hadn't found the time to pay his bills in a very long time—so long in fact that most of the distributors in town had the contractor's account on COD (cash on delivery). As much as the sale rep wanted to help me, he couldn't, not until the account was brought current.

So I went back to the contractor's office and asked the nice accounting person about what I was just told by the vender. She politely directed me to go see the person in the trailer adjacent to the office, whose title, other than new wife of owner, I wasn't sure of at the time.

Knocking on the door as I walked in the trailer, I said "Hello!" and officially introduced myself even though she already knew who I was. I then asked if she had a minute.

Sitting down across the desk from her, I proceeded to tell her about my encounter with the vender's sales rep. As I was speaking, I noticed she was not interested much in what I was saying as she continued the work on whatever it was prior to my entering her office.

After I was done, and showing little concern about what I had just told her, she very nonchalantly pointed my attention to two relatively large moving boxes in the corner of her office. As I looked closer, I saw that both boxes were filled to the top with payable checks attached to vender and/or subcontractor statements dating back months. By all indications, not only did it appear she was in charge of keeping an eye on the bank account, but she was also the final stop for when any monies would actually be distributed to venders and subcontractors.

She then told me that all the venders would eventually get paid in due time, but for now, I would have to use the one vender that the owner of the company had designated to keep current for all project managers and estimators to use. She told me who the vender was and off I went.

Progressive, "high performance" companies understand the importance of managing their cash flow. They know the effects it has on their operation's ability to perform at peak efficiency, as well as their ability to invest back into the operation in terms of upgrades to their plant, equipment, and personnel training. And because of this, they are keenly aware of who in the company has the greatest influence over whether the company's cash flow continues to trend in a positive or negative direction at any given time.

Time for a Mental Note

The definition of revenue, or, when revenues can be recognized, is by no means universally accepted. Although the health of a company's revenue is one of the most important aspects a business needs to measure, monitor, and evaluate in order to meet future obligations, guidance of when revenue is allowed to be recognized differs between the two standard bearers of accounting principles and guidelines, GAAP and IFRS (International Financial Reporting Standards).

In an effort to maximize the health of their revenue streams, "high performance" companies constantly seek the upper limit of any benefit (return) to be gained throughout the entire spectrum of a financial transaction. "High performance" companies also recognize the fact that healthy revenues are not limited to historical paradigms, processes, data, or results as most business owners, executives and entrepreneurs are compelled to believe these days. "High performance" companies know that the health of their anticipated revenue stream is not born on the day a contract or purchase agreement gets awarded, but rather, healthy revenue streams are created, i.e., developed, over the entire course the transactional process, right up to the point the last dollar of revenue is collected.

If you were to ask anyone of a multitude of business owners, executives, or entrepreneurs in operation today about the health of their revenue stream, most would respond by typically saying that their backlog is either "good" or "cheap," never in terms of whether it's healthy or unhealthy. Obviously to most business owners, executives, and entrepreneurs, the difference between "good" and "cheap" depends on what stage the transactional process is in when the question gets asked. If the transactional process is at a mature stage, business owners, executives, and entrepreneurs will typically equate their answer to how much anticipated profit was being projected once the process was complete. Lots of profit mean "good," limited or no amount profits means "cheap." Simple, but not very insightful or informative about the entire transactional process.

In all reality, the vast majority of business owners, executives, or entrepreneurs have absolutely no idea, within a 10 percent + or − deviation, whether or not their transactional process is truly "good" or "cheap," "healthy" or "unhealthy." The reason for this is because they constantly fail to recognize the fact that profit projections are only as accurate as the people providing the information. If managers and/or supervisor haven't been properly trained about the importance of managing cash flow, it is ludicrous for any business owners, executives, or entrepreneurs to believe that the profit projections being provided by them from one month to the next will even come close to reflecting the reality of the situation. In fact, chances are that the ongoing transactional process, i.e., deliverables, is so inefficient, that each day that goes by less and less profit is being generated or maintained, meaning it's being lost.

Background: Tampa, FL

In 2016, I was with a large specialty contracting company who at the time just landed a large subcontract with a long time customer to install a raceway system on a new guideway that was being built at the international airport. Although the work was negotiated with a reasonable profit margin, it was still going to be a very difficult project to deliver in the allotted time.

As time passed, we started to see additional design changes that required pricing. Moreover, although we had mobilized to the site, it became apparent that the project's schedule had slipped somewhere between three and four months; which also raised concerns since there was the threat of liquidated damages being assessed at the end of the project for late delivery. Eventually, we were able to conclude what our actual scope was going to be and began to install the work.

As the work progressed on the eight month project, we started to see the potential of a much larger return (profit) being generated. Our crews were installing the raceway system at a much faster rate than originally anticipated, plus, during the renegotiations of the scope and price, additional profits had been potential generated from a paper point of view.

About halfway through the project, we noticed that reimbursements from our monthly payment applications started to get delayed. Without any type of reasonable explanation from our customer, we continued to submit subsequent payment applications each month that reflected work installed during that period of time. Eventually, senior management for both companies got involved and it was disclosed by the customer that they had not been paid by their customer due to disputes with their performance, and since our contract with the customer contained a "Pay when Paid" clause, our customer was not compelled to pull monies out of their own pocket and pay us, even though we were not the cause of their dispute with their customer. And because of their dispute with their customer, there was no telling, if or when, we would see our reimbursement for the work.

Time for a Mental Note

Contractors should be aware of the fact that just because you expect to make a profit at the end of a project doesn't necessarily mean you will ever collect it. Moreover, when anticipated levels of revenue become less likely to be collected, added encumbrances (i.e., costs for attorneys, etc.) required to collect the monies owed automatically have a negative impact to the health of a contractor's previously reported earned revenue.

Contrary to popular belief, business owners, executives, or entrepreneurs should never feel comfortable predicting at the start of a transactional process whether the ensuing revenue stream is either "good" or "cheap," "healthy" or "unhealthy." Why? Because in order to be accurate, the dimension of "time" must be applied to the process.

In math and science, "time" is often referred to as the fourth dimension. In business, "time" is relative to the period between when a proposal is accepted by a customer and any given point along the transactional process time continuum. It's relative because the anticipated health of the revenue stream can be impacted for various reasons along the way, both positively and negatively. Again, healthy revenues are never born, they're created over time.

Make no mistake about it; it takes a considerable amount of effort from the beginning of a transactional process to the last dollar being collected in order to legitimately increase the health of an anticipated revenue stream. And because most business owners, executives, or entrepreneurs are unable to continually monitor the relative value or costs to effectively manage a transactional process, it makes it very difficult for them to accept a more advanced and intensified way of managing their deliverables to customers.

However, if your goal as a future business owner, executive, or entrepreneur is to reap the benefits from operating a progressive, "high performance" company, there is absolutely no getting around the effort required to create healthy streams of revenue through the entire transactional process.

CHAPTER
14

Conflict and Negotiations

As most people who watch the news on TV, or read online, will tell you, it seems just about everyone these days has some sort of grievance or conflict with another part. Road rage incidents, immigrants trying to enter the country illegally, lobbyists trying to get some form of legislation passed, financial transaction gone awry, lien against property, divorce, harassment suit, wrongful death or injury, someone allegedly broke the law, you name it there's an attorney close by to lend his or her services.

Think about this statistic for a second. According to the American Bar Association there are at least 1.1 million attorneys practicing law in the US today. With approximately 320 million people living in the US that means for every three hundred or so people there's at least one attorney potentially billing a customer each and every day. And although two-thirds of the attorneys are male, roughly 90 percent of all attorneys in the US are Caucasian, a fact I find interesting when over 30 percent of the population is minority.

With so many attorneys at one's disposal, is there any wonder why there are so many conflicts going on in the world from one day to the next?

Whether you are working in an office or providing a service in the field, there is no other industry or profession like construction where someone can get their competitive juices flowing just about any time of the day. In fact, not only are conflicts and disputes a common occurrence in most industries like construction, but the communication process by which conflicts are resolved is often times colorful and expressed in some of the most interesting terms and words.

For future business owners, executives, and entrepreneurs considering careers in industries like construction where written agreements are the norm and not the exception, it's important to note that the very essence of every business transaction is governed and/or controlled by an agreement between at least two parties. And more often than not, the interpretation of what is contained in these agreements, whether expressly written or latently intended to be, becomes the source of every dispute between parties.

Time for a Mental Note

Conflicts, differing opinions, and confrontations are a part of most industries like construction where competition is its cornerstone. Those who do not embrace this fact, or are prepared to engage in it, more times than not will find themselves coming up on the short end of a negotiated settlement.

From a conventional perspective, most would view conflict as a protracted, and possibly heated, disagreement, or argument between at least two parties where subsequent negotiations take on a more civil tone when a mutually beneficial outcome is eventually deemed appropriate. As nice as this scenario may fit most professions when the discussion of conflict and conflict resolution arises, it is far from the realities of what folks in competitive industries like construction go through as a normal course of business.

As in life, the more aggressive and pressing one becomes in order to get his or her own way, the more likely that person will end up coming away with the majority of what he or she was expecting to receive from a negotiations prior to any conflict beginning. Why?

Because most rationale people tend to be of a passive nature and shy away from conflict.

Granted, no one likes a bully, abuser, or aggressive person for that matter; and we universally agree that no form of violence can ever be tolerated. But to many, conflict is a vital function in life's pursuit of progress, clarity, exceptionalism, and sustainability. Conflict also allows for two opposing points of view to be exercised in the hope that a better outcome would result well beyond any stated position or claim. In other words, 2 + 2 equals something greater than 4, which is also the basis for the interdependent concept of "synergy" as we all know.

For me, this chapter of the book is probably one of the most important dynamics of business, and in life for that matter, future generations of business owners, executives, and entrepreneurs will need to grasp and fully comprehend if they ever plan to succeed at what they so.

Today, "pop culture" and the political divide of an ever-entrenched two-party system in the US is weaponizing what used to be a peaceful disputes resolution process among opposing parties in pursuant of a mutually beneficial outcome in order to score political and ideological points with society at large. And through this weaponization process, the art of effectively negotiating any type of settlement gets immediately drowned out and eventually lost by all the violent hate laced rhetoric that gets exchange as combatants talk past one another.

Just look around college campuses these days as ask yourself if progress is truly being made to develop the future business leaders, executives, and entrepreneurs when "safe places" and "snowflakes" abound. What you find is students of all ages cowering under to the pressure of (a) someone complaining that they didn't receive and an award even though they lost a contest, (b) someone raising their voice, (c) someone aggressively pushing a position in order reach a consensus, or (d) someone expressing an opposing viewpoints. The simple fact that liberal minded free thinkers are now promoting the notion that everyone gets an award just for participating is in no way preparing anyone for the harsh realities of the business world.

So why is the discussion about conflict an important one to have? Here is one of many reasons:

Background: Los Angeles, CA

Remember the hotel renovation project I told you about in an earlier chapter? If you will recall, I was actually the second project manager the electrical contractor hired because the first one did not have the necessary experience to oversee the size and complexity of the project. Besides not having an experienced project manager to oversee the project, the electrical contractor was also very skeptical about the capabilities of the senior general foreman he put in charge to manage the field forces.

On the drive to the site my first day as an employee, the owner of the company proudly informed me that it was his project manager (my predecessor who was anxiously awaiting to turn the project over to someone else) who was the one who actually brought the large renovation project opportunity in the table. The owner also told me that the project manager was the one who eventually took the lead on putting together all of the scopes and electrical budgets for the project; which I found somewhat odd given the massive size of the renovation and new electrical work being required for a commercial installation when the project manager's entire experience had supposedly been in industrial work.

Arriving at the site around 9:30 AM, the owner and I made our way to the site office through the massive rooms and colonnades with their high ceilings and spectacular architectural features. As it turns out, the first familiar person we ran into was the outgoing project manager who appeared looking extremely worn down for so early in the morning. Although pleasant, he didn't smile much, nor did it appear he was dressed in the appropriate attire to leave the office much, perform site inspections, or at the very least give the owner and me a tour of the project.

It didn't take long before both the owner and project manager started describing to me the various scopes of the renovation project.

It was a massive undertaking to say the least, and it didn't take long for me to figure out why he was hired in the first place, and, why the owner was so concerned about how the project had been managed by the current project manager up to that point.

Technically, the project manager was as sharp as any electrician in the business, but all too often, like most contractors, the owner fell into the trap of thinking that since a proven field supervisor has the necessary skills to lead an installation, he or she should be able to also handle, without any additional formal training, project management requirements that deal with both business and administrative concerns. This particular field supervisor turn project manager appeared on the surface to have little to no training on how to handle a construction project from a business or administrative perspective.

As the explanations and overview continued by both the owner and project manager, I was immediately struck by how much the owner actually knew about the $250 million renovation and office tower addition project, down to almost every detail of the electrical scope of work. This also told me that the owner had more involvement in the development of the project than he had been letting on. Then, the owner asked the project manager to radio ahead to the senior general foreman in charge of the project—who we eventually met up with on the upper guest room floors where construction had already been well under way for months. Needless to say the project manager did not join us for the project tour.

Making our way back out of the construction office area, I can remember the owner passionately expressing his joy at being a part of such a historic project. To him, it was the project of a life-time, and he was going to do everything he could to make it a huge success for his relatively new company.

Stopping at one of the empty guest rooms under construction and walking in, I noticed the expression on the owners face quickly turn to one of concern as he started closely looking at the demolition and rough-in work that had been already completed. With a brief, "Huh!" he walked past and out of the room he went.

Walking a step or two behind the owner and to his side, I noticed the owner kept looking side to side into each guest room as the pace of his walk started to accelerate slightly. Then suddenly, he took an abrupt turn into one of the guest rooms as if he noticed something.

As I walked in behind the owner, I noticed that construction activities were still very much underway, unlike the previous guestroom which appeared to have been freshly swept and ready for plaster patching and finishes. No one was in the guest room when we arrived, however, it was obvious that someone had been chiseling the sixty-year-old plaster because you could see piles of debris all along the baseboard of the wall.

Armed with a number of small rolls of drawings under his arm, the owner's middle aged senior general foreman happened to find us somehow in and amongst the 1440 guest rooms being renovated. A seemingly timid and reserved individual, slight of build, and reasonably shorter than the owner and me.

After introductions and a brief history of the senior general foreman's relationship with the owner, the owner asked him to describe the installation and construction sequence taking place in the typical guest rooms. Once the senior general foreman concluded, the owner decided that he wanted to keep walking in order to see how progress was being made throughout the floor based on the senior general foreman's explanation he just provided.

As the walk-through of the floor continued, it appeared the owner started stopping into more and more at each guest rooms checking to see if the installation sequence was consistent with what the senior general foreman had described. Running out of guest rooms on the floors to inspect, the owner asked the senior general foreman to take us down to the level where the early demolition work in the guest rooms was just beginning.

Arriving just one floor down from where we were, the owner asked the senior general foreman to take us to a guest room that demolition was just starting.

Walking into a dusty guest room, the owner turned to his senior general foreman and asked him to describe in much greater detail the sequence of work. However, this time the owner wanted to know at what state of demolition was the electrical scope of work supposed to begin.

Appearing somewhat perplexed, not to mention oblivious, about the actual details of the construction sequence, and not knowing where the owner was going with this particular line of questioning, it became painfully obvious to me that the owner knew something that the senior general foreman wasn't telling him. I then remembered just how much the owner actually knew about the project as I listened to the project manager and him describe in minute detail the various scopes of the electrical contract while standing the site office downstairs. So I quickly stepped back a few steps and turned to the side not sure what was about to happen.

Then I heard the owner in a stern voice ask the senior general foreman if he had brought with him the drawings for the typical guest rooms. As it turned out, the small rolls he had been carrying under his arm were the typical guest room drawings.

Stepping to the side of the senior general foreman, and grabbing the edge of the drawings, the owner asked to see the general construction notes and details, not the electrical scope of work notes and details.

Reading the notes intently, the owner stops, looks up, and started pointing around the room to all the chiseling and channeling of the sixty-plus-year-old plaster walls that had electrical raceway already installed. The owner then asked the question, "Who is doing all of this chiseling and channeling?"

It was at that point when the senior general foreman used the words "our guys" and quickly added that the chiseling and channeling was taking an enormous amount of time to do. Seconds later, and in fit of rage, the owner took all the drawings and threw them against the wall, accompanied by a number of expletives. He then instructed the senior general foreman to get on the radio and have the project manager get up to the guest room.

Still seething from what he had just heard, the owner reached down and gathered up the drawings. Trying to get his composer back, the owner aggressively scrolled through the now dust ladened drawings searching for the sheet that contained the notes he had just read. Finding the sheet, he pointing angrily at the note that read "All demolition to be performed by the general contractor." Then, without hesitation, the owner made it abundantly clear to everyone in the room that demolition of the walls was not part of the electrical scope of work and unless a change order had been previously negotiated between the project manager and owner/developer, who was also acting as his own general contractor, the senior general foreman and his crews should not been spending any time or money performing the work.

Hoping against hope that the project manager had negotiated a change order to do the chiseling and channeling of the walls, several minutes had passed before the project manager eventually graced us with his presence. Slowing sauntering in through doorway the project manager asked, "What's going on?"

In a calm but stern voice, the owner looked at the project manager asked if he knew what was going on with regards to the demolition. Sensing he had better answer the question correctly by the way the owner was looking at him, not to mention the terrified look on the senior general foreman's face which was on full display, the project manager replied that it was something he was looking into. And the reason for the delay was due to the fact that since the owner/developer was acting as his own general contractor, he hadn't quite gotten all of his resources up to speed yet, so in the interim, given the fact electricians were wasting time and money standing around waiting for the general contractor to chisel and channel the plaster walls, the senior general foreman took upon himself to start putting crews to work performing the general contractor's scope.

Upon hearing the project manager's explanation, the owner then asked both the project manager and senior project manager to show him how all the added costs for the demolition were being tracked in case a deal couldn't be worked out and the owner/developer needed to write them a change order for the costs that had already been incurred. At that moment, the project manager and senior general foreman looked at one another as to say, "You got this?"

Livid at the prospect of having countless dollars at risk, the owner then asked the senior general foreman if he knew what the scope of the electrical work was. He responded that he only knows what he has been told by the project manager and the general contractor's superintendent. He then went onto say that he had not been given a copy of the subcontract, proposal letter, or a list of inclusions and exclusions to review. When asked by the owner how long had the chiseling and channeling been going on, the senior general foreman responded that they had almost completed 4 complete floors out of the fourteen floors, or approximately four hundred rooms.

Needless to say, there was no more chiseling, channeling, or cleanup performed by the electrical contractor's crews.

Sadly, this type of conflict from a contractual perspective and emotional outburst, along with substantial losses that followed, happens all the time in business, not just construction. But what is most perplexing to me is the fact that these types of conflicts, emotional outbursts, and losses of profit are totally avoidable so long as everyone is willing to deal with the realities of the situation and not deflect or misrepresent the facts at hand.

To me, conflict is the necessary precursor to achieving something that possess greater "value." Greater "value" for those opposing one another as well as those who get caught up in the wake of an ultimate agreement. Moreover, if one were to truly take a step back and look at the entire process of conflict resolution in its purist form, putting aside any bravado being generated from either side, they would find themselves taking a fascinating journey of human emotions bound by the two ever-present guiderails found in every negotiations, "leverage" and "weakness" of position.

Background: Denver, CO

In the early 1990s, I found myself doing a considerable amount of traveling between Kansas City and Denver as a VP for a large regional specialty contractor. And as with most air travel, at some point frequent fliers will reach down into the seat pocket in front of them to glance through the updated airline magazine that typically comes out the first of every month in order to pass the time away. I was no different.

With each flight to and from Denver at the first of each month, I would routinely reach for the airline's magazine in the seat pocket ahead of me. And without exception, each time I would open up the magazine an embedded advertisement from Karrass negotiating seminars would be the first thing I would see. Initially, I would be both annoyed and curious at the same time. I would get annoyed thinking about the repetitive nature of the whole experience, having to look at the advertisement the very second I opened up the magazine, but curious at what seemed on the surface to be a very expensive, but captive, marketing campaign.

Then one day, on one of my trips, I was accompanied by a senior executive of the company who told me that we would be meeting with a nationwide vender on this trip in the hopes of settling some outstanding payable issues. What I wasn't told prior to the meeting was the fact that we had been in a conflict with this particular vender for quite some time now and negotiations hadn't been going so well as of late.

Introduced as the new VP of Operations for the Denver-based branch, no one from the vender's side of the table seemed to be the least bit impressed. All the vender's senior executives wanted to know was when they were going to receive payment for their long overdue invoices. Like a deer in the headlights, I responded by saying something to the effect that I couldn't give them an answer right then and there, but I would certainly look into it and get back with them. Then, the meeting abruptly ended with what appeared to me doing nothing more than exacerbating the situation by my answer.

After the meeting, I wasn't agitated about the fact that I was just injected into a possible claims or litigation discussion. I was actually more concerned about my own lack of knowledge to deal with such a high stakes situation like the one I had just encountered. It was at that point I knew I needed to get educated, and quickly, because these guys were not going away any time soon. So I started searching for ways to do just that in the shortest amount of time.

Time for a Mental Note

You may remember me telling you the story of my first encounter with a claim situation, which took place about seven years earlier in Los Angeles when the specialty contractor I was with at the time was dismissed from a large project because he wouldn't renegotiate his fee structure. That was the only other time in my young career in construction that I was close to any claims situation. However, in that case, although I was the Sr. Project Manager in charge of the project, once I had provided all the supporting documentation to the owner and his attorney, I basically become nothing more than a bystander to all the subsequent conversations and/or negotiations between the opposing parties.

Since that time in Los Angeles, until my fateful trip to Denver to meet with the hostile vender, I had not found myself in any situation that remotely resembled what I had just went through. Any conflict or dispute that may have occurred prior to this time was resolved at the project level in what I thought was a fair and equitable manner. So to be made part of something of this magnitude was totally foreign to me, and quite frankly, other than having a competitive nature, I had absolutely no previous direction on how to successfully navigate my way through a conflict resolution process.

During the ensuing weeks, negotiations between the specialty contractor and the vender continued to decay with no clear resolution on the horizon. Eventually, it was agreed by both parties that the next round of discussions would take place at the vendor's corporate offices located in the St. Louis area with everyone's legal counsel being invited.

Still nowhere near prepared to handle the negotiations, I agreed to go to the meeting in St. Louis armed with our own attorney accompanying me on the trip. A person I had not met prior. All I was ever told about the attorney by my senior management was that he came with the reputation of being a "bulldog" and things would go just fine.

On the flight over to St. Louis, our attorney and I made sure we had seats next to one another so we could better prepare for what was about to happen. Not long into our conversation, it became obvious to me that the attorney had a wealth of experience dealing with these types of situations. Then it dawned on me that he might think I too had similar negotiating experiences and I need to make sure he knew that I hadn't in order to avoid a potentially disastrous outcome later that day.

As the negotiations got underway, I quickly picked up on the fact that to our attorney none of this was personal. He never interrupted the vender or vender's legal counsel, nor did he ever not look at the person speaking, except may be for a brief moment to jot down a note or two. In the end, I found myself becoming more of a student than an officer of the company I was representing.

To a naive and inexperienced negotiator such as myself, our attorney was a master, systematically creating leverage points along the way against the opposing counsel by using complementary expressions like: "You're smarter than that!" or "Being an attorney, I'm not telling you anything you don't already know." What also struck me about our attorney was the fact he never seemed to negotiate against himself, or lose his temper.

Whenever there came a time during the negotiations for a commercial offer to be put on the table, our attorney would not be the first to do so. He would patiently sit back, shut his mouth, and wait. If for whatever an offer from the other side didn't come, he would skillfully let the other side believe that by them not putting the first offer on the table, all it was going to do was extend the time it was going to take for them to get a check (which he knew was their ultimate motivation that day).

After watching the attorney's masterful performance during the negotiations, and seeing how he continually negotiated for the last right of refusal, it didn't take long for me to get hooked. To me, it was as if Picasso was painting a masterpiece; and all I wanted do from that point forward was learn how to paint. Needless to say, I couldn't wait to get my hands on that Karrass advertisement and signed up for the next multi-day seminar.

Time for a Mental Note

"In business as in life, you don't get what you deserve, you get what you negotiate." (Chester L. Karrass)

It is a simple fact that if you want to survive and succeed in any industry at the highest operational levels, you have to know how to negotiate. Whether you're maneuvering for the last right of refusal during contract talks, or trying to resolve a conflict offsite or in the office, the need to be an effective negotiator is paramount if one desires a favorable outcome more often than not.

Here is a list of salient negotiating points that I've come to understand, appreciate, and put into practice over the course of my career that should be helpful to every business owner, executive, and entrepreneur going forward:

- Try to set the ground rules for any negotiations prior to discussions starting. Make it known that you are seeking a mutually beneficial "Win-Win" outcome if at all possible.
- Always negotiate for the last right of refusal.
- Never make negotiations personal. Keep everyone's focus on the contributing elements of the problem, never the person.
- Never go into a negotiations with a preconceived deal already embedded in your mind; especially one that is based upon only getting reimbursed for what something 'Costs'. You must always keep in mind that it's not what something "costs" that is important, it's what you can sell it for. Getting someone to *buy* what something "costs" presents no significant challenge to the seller; however, getting someone to *pay* for "value" is well worth the seller's effort.
- Never go into a negotiations tired or unrested. The human body, especially the mind, wears down over time. Rest and/or sleep are the best remedy for a tired mind and body.

- Never get into a position where you have to make the first offer of any negotiations unless, you are already at a serious disadvantage and you need a starting point for negotiations to continue because you never know what the other party is thinking in terms of what's a fair and/or reasonable settlement. Also too, during the early part of a negotiation, it may be too soon to know what the actual motivating factors might be of the opposing party. Eventually, over time, and as discussion unfold, if you are patient and listen carefully, the opposing parties' motivating factors will come to light.

- Know when not to have the ultimate authority at the table. Just the mere presence of mind that you will have to take a tentative agreement up the ladder often times turns out to be very beneficial to the party who reserves their right for last right of refusal.

- Always try and establish a pecking order and characteristics of your negotiating team. It is important to have a "good cop"/"bad cop" scenario in order to maximize the outcome of any negotiations.

- Discipline yourself, and others accompanying your team, not to say too much, chances are the other side is listening to every work you say as intently as you are trying to do. Loose lips definitely sink ships during high stakes negotiations, and those who tend to talk more are obviously listening less to the opposing party.

- If a negotiation has multiple parts, try not to take each one totally off the table as they get resolved. You may have to pull some of them back as a "throw-away" in order to reach a better settlement on a future one(s).

- You have to first understand that every negotiation is a contest between competing motivations, and once you understand the motivation of your opponent, only then do you have the ability to reach the most favorable outcome to yourself.

- Negotiations involve the interaction between individual personalities, i.e., "values," beliefs, and attitudes which have been formed over many years; and knowing the personality of the opposing party is paramount to achieving a favorable outcome.

- Negotiations are a dynamic process that at times is unpredictable. You may think you have your opponent's strategy figured out, only to discover at some point that their position on a particular topic has changed—i.e., gotten harder or softer, along with their tactics. Good negotiators are always prepared to pivot to a supplemental strategy.

- You have to be patient and keep digging to find out what's the true story behind the motivation of the opposing side. Some of the worst, or most lopsided, deals are those resulting from one party not willing to take the time to understand the opponent's side of the story. Speeding up a negotiation tends to favor the party not in a hurry to make a deal.

- In every negotiation there exists a linear relationship between the outcome of the negotiations and the amount of leverage created by one party over the other. As leverage increases over the opposing party, so too, does the chances of a favorable outcome for the party creating the highest degree of leverage.

- Never be afraid to ask for a caucus during times of negotiations. Because negotiations are a dynamic process, those who keep their heads and are able to regroup in middle of a discussion usually find themselves in a more favorable position, post-caucus, as opposed to trying to grind through a negotiation session.

- Never be afraid to use the tactic of walking away from the table when negotiations have either stalled, or, don't seem to be going in a direction preferable to your liking.

Background: Atlanta, GA

The company I was with at the time was in the midst of negotiating a design-assist/lump sum contract with an international manufacturer who had been recently awarded a multimillion dollar traction power, e.g., transit, related prime contract. Even though the manufacturer had already secured the prime contract, we were continually being asked by them to price changes that adversely affected the electrical, communication, and signaling scopes of work.

With the start of construction looming, pricing and subsequent negotiations were not progressing as expected. For appearance sake, everyone knew it was important that the project got started on time, especially with a $25,000 per day liquidated damages (LDs) clause if the project didn't finish on time. But for whatever reason, LDs didn't seem to matter to the manufacturer. In the spirit of good faith, my group VP agreed to have our team start mobilize to the site which was approximately five hundred miles away from our home office.

Over the next sixty days, and six figures worth of mobilization costs already committed, my group VP and I tried in earnest to get to a number everyone could live with for the most current scope of wok the manufacture had on the table. Being the on-site senior contract manager, it was my job to get the negotiations to a point where the company could still make a reasonable profit given the amount of risk they were about to incur over the next year and a half. From there, any modifications would have to be signed off by my group VP.

By this time, well over two years had passed since we submitted our original pricing to the manufacturer in support of our bid, and as a consequence, our original commodity pricing was no longer valid, which didn't seem to concern the manufacturer because he continued to reject any increases to our unit prices. Moreover, qualified labor in the local market was becoming depleted due to the market experiencing economic expansion to the point where it appeared the market was going to be at full employment within months, and continue to be that way for at least the next few years.

Watching all of these negative impacts to our pricing continue to pile up to the tune of multiple seven figures, our group VP and senior members of the manufacturer's procurement staff finally agreed to meet face-to-face in an effort to resolve the pricing differences in the hope of getting to a final contract.

At the meeting, each side laid out their concerns and issues, however, neither side showed a willingness early on to give up much of anything; and understandably so, given the fact that my group VP was facing serious impacts to a two-year-old estimate, and the customer was facing his own budgetary constraints as well. At one point, it didn't look like much of anything was going to come out of the negotiations.

Then, in the middle of it all, I remembered something that the Karrass seminar taught me, and that was, when both sides seem to get to an impasse, take a break and talk amongst yourselves. But also too, try not to let the other side know why you are initiating a break in the action, hopefully, they'll think you are about to concede a point or two when you get back to the table; and in doing so, they'll actually be ready to counter themselves if you can get them to speak first and make the first offer.

After two caucuses each side returned to the negotiating table with no movement or concession. Then, our group VP had had enough and announced to everyone that if the customer (manufacturer) was unwilling to come to a reasonable agreement, they could take the project and contract back, and we would forgo doing the project.

Somewhat stunned by the announcement, the customer's procurement staff quickly asked for a third caucus because they knew from past experience contractors never consider walking away from a negotiated design/assist project the size of this one without good reason. But they feared we might, given the state of the discussions.

Returning to the table and unsure if the group VP was serious or not, the customer once again pushed back on the group VP by saying they really couldn't concede to anything else, however, it was their desire to reach a mutually beneficial agreement and not have us pull off the project. In response, the group VP said in a calm voice, "Well then, it looks like we won't be doing this job together."

Now, I have been in some tough negotiations before with other customers, contractors, bankers, and attorneys, but I don't think I would have ever had the nerve to offer up an eight digit contract without considerably more deliberations taking place. But when the customer returned to the table for what turned out to be the last time, the group VP had no compunction about walking away (another Karrass technique for effective negotiating); and the rest was history. We ended up with the contract based on the group VP's final number, terms, and conditions.

Without question, all of the bullet points I listed above have proven effective over the years, but the one I've discovered time and again to be THE most important is the one that identifies the concept of negotiations as being the interaction between individual personalities, i.e., "values," beliefs, and attitudes, which have been formed over many years. Knowing, or discovering, the personality traits of the opposing party is paramount to achieving a favorable outcome.

We can all agree that people have differing personality traits based on "values," beliefs, and attitudes. Formed shortly after birth, and influenced throughout life's journey of trials, tribulations, and successes, right up to the age of about twenty. Then, as if nature flips a switch, individual personality traits become somewhat locked in, rigid, and definable. At which point, individual personality profiles can be deduced for future reference using specific parameters.

Time for a Mental Note

A personality profile is also a tool that can be used by the management structure of an organization in order to evaluate an employee's personal skills, "values," beliefs, and attitudes in an effort to maximize their workplace performance.

So why are personality profiles, i.e., "values" beliefs, and attitudes, so important to know about prior to or during a negotiations?

Short answer: Knowing personality profiles are key to resolving any conflict to the mutual benefit of all parties, whether the environment is business or personal.

In business, as we all know, there can be any number of conflicts, and conflict resolutions, i.e., negotiations, taking place at any given time that involve a whole host of different entities at odds with one another. Conflicts that usually get resolved to the mutual benefit of all parties, but there are definitely those that truly never get resolved, leaving behind hard feeling and a dysfunctional work environment that affects both employees and customers alike.

As the generational gaps in the US continue to get wider as the older generations live and work longer, understanding personality traits and profiles is going to play an important role more than ever before, especially when "values" beliefs, and attitudes start to collide in a hierarchical structure where the culture of the company is void of any operational alignment and synergy. Future business owners, executives, entrepreneurs have to understand this if they ever want to reach the level of a progressive, "high performance" company.

If you believe as I do that conflict, conflict resolution, and negotiations involve the interaction between long engrained individual personality traits, then it would hold true that once a dispute arises between opposing parties there is no guaranty that a resolution might ever be reached, or, one that doesn't require a third party to render a binding decision. All the more reason why future business owners, executives, and entrepreneurs must regularly ask themselves this two-part question about every candidate for employment:

a)   What is the personality profile of the candidate?
b)   Does the position slotted for the employee match with the candidate's personality profile?

All too often in today's business environment, most business owners, executives, and entrepreneurs could care less about a candidate's, or existing employee's for that matter, personality profile when it comes to filling a position. All that usually matters these days is whether or not a candidate comes with a positive or negative reference from previous employers. A hiring criteria that I think is truly a big mistake.

Assuming a candidate has the requisite capabilities, what most business owners, executives, and entrepreneurs today will eventually tell you is that what matters most to them during the hiring process is a determination being reached as to how well a prospective employee can be trusted to look after the betterment of the company, not if the candidate's personality profile matches the job description. In other words, most business owners, executives, and entrepreneurs today are more concerned about whether or not an employee will steal from them, or lie to them, as opposed to whether or not the employee can actually do the job at a high level, and, add "value" to the company.

Time for a Mental Note

Jack Welch, ex-CEO of GE, has famously promoted the idea that all employees of an organization can be divided up in the following four categories:

a) High performer: an employee that buys into the corporate culture, and as a result, should be promoted and empowered as much as possible.
b) Low performer: an employee that doesn't buy into the corporate culture, and as a result, should be fired as quickly as possible.
c) Low performer: an employee that buys into the corporate culture, and as a result, should be given a second chance and placed in a different position to see if they can eventually become high performers.
d) High performer: an employee that doesn't buy into the corporate culture, and as a result, should be fired immediately and made an example out of by discussing with other managers why specific attitudes will not be tolerated in the organization.

Without question, progressive "high performance" companies are constantly evaluating the caliber of their employees, not just managers and supervisors, but all employee. As a result, progressive, "high performance" companies are better able to know: (a) which employee may need additional training in order to achieve higher standards of performance; (b) which employee may have exceeded performance expectations and is ready for additional responsibilities; and (c) which employees may need to be offered up to the industry due consistently poor performance reviews, or, an inability to conform to the organization's culture.

If you really want to know how to operationally align a business with maximum synergy throughout the entire organization structure, you first have to scrap any notion that staff positions within an organizational structure are created for people before anything else. Why? Because an organizational structure is created for one reason and one reason only, and that's to support the business purpose, i.e., business plan, not to randomly place employees who may or may not provide the adequate "value" required by the company or its customers.

Operational alignment begins with a business plan and ends with qualified employees being strategically placed in an organizational structure to add "value" to the company as a whole. Here's what I mean:

- Step 1 of any business purpose is the development of a business plan that lays out the foundational belief and vision of "why" the company exists in its present form.
- Step 2 of any business purpose is to create the necessary operational systems in support of the business plan. It's the "how" a company fulfills its foundational belief and vision.
- Step 3 of any business purpose is to create an organizational structure that supports the operational systems that have been established to support the business plan.
- Step 4 of any business purpose is strategically staff the organizational structure with competent employees who can add "value" to the company going forward.

- Step 5 of any business purpose is to continually provide training to all employees in effort to show them how to provide "value" beyond just being a good employee that has mastered the performance standards established for the position they were hired to occupy.

To be a progressive "high performance" company, personnel decisions can never be considered personal. I realize that may sound a bit oxymoronic, but "for profit" organizations are not established to operate as charities. Why? Because in charitable organizations, unlike "for profit" organizations like contracting, employees are usually volunteers where job performance is not a determining factor for being a part of an organization structure. Charitable organizations are also where the morale of others, i.e., co-workers, plays a less important role to the overall alignment and synergy of the organizational structure.

Over my career, I have hired and/or managed thousands of employees, and just because someone appears to be trustworthy, doesn't necessarily mean they are. Not only can this lack of behavioral awareness of an employee cost unsuspecting companies latent amounts of money on a regular basis, but it can also put a company's mere existence in jeopardy to a point where some of the damage caused by less than desirable employees is irreversible.

Time for Mental Note

The headline of an article written in the *Guardian* and published on February 24, 2015, read: "Barings collapse at 20: How rogue trader Nick Leeson broke the bank."

This is how the rest of the article read:

> *Twenty years ago, Nick Leeson caused the collapse of Barings, the City's oldest merchant bank and banker to the Queen*

Nick Leeson on banking: extremely competitive…and improperly policed

In his autobiography Rogue Trader, Nick Leeson said the ethos at Barings was simple: 'We were all driven to make profits, profits, and more profits… I was the rising star.'

Leeson did make Barings vast sums. In 1993, he made £10m—10% of the bank's profits for that year. But in 1995, the discovery of a secret file—Error Account 88888—showed that Leeson had gambled away £827m in Barings's name.

The City's oldest merchant bank was finished.

As stock markets took fright from the biggest financial scandal in years, Watford born Leeson fled the firm's Singapore office leaving a note saying 'I'm sorry'. He then went on the run.

In his absence, a mixed picture emerged of the 28-year-old whose golden touch in the currency market earned him £200,000 a year. Some colleagues said he was 'brilliant' and the 'most confident' trader in town'. *Others said he was a 'high-flyer who liked to dabble in dare-devil trades.'*

With a global manhunt underway, Leeson surprised everyone by turning up at Frankfurt airport *several days later. He then began a nine month battle to avoid extradition to Singapore, which failed.*

Almost a year after fleeing Singapore, Leeson landed at Changi airport *escorted by security. Wearing gym gear and a baseball cap turned back to front, he looked relaxed. He was charged with forgery and fraud in relation to the collapse of Barings.*

At his trial at Singapore District Court, Leeson, who had been held at Tanah Merah maximum security prison, admitted charges of forgery and cheating. Presumably in an attempt to play the sympathy card, his lawyer told the court that Leeson

had said his wife had suffered a miscarriage and that Leeson was financially ruined. Unmoved, the judge sentenced Leeson to 6 ½ years in prison.

The risk of a longer prison sentence put Leeson off appealing, instead he served four years in a Singapore jail. During his spell in prison he was diagnosed with colon cancer for which he received treatment. In 1999, Leeson was freed and enjoyed champagne and smoked salmon *on the flight back to London with British journalists.*

Such was the interest in Leeson's remarkable story the Sunday Mirror reported that he had made £200,000 from a book deal and a newspaper serialisation. He also received a share of the £7m profit from the film Rogue Trader, which stared Ewan McGregor and Anna Friel.

As for Barings, it become part of ING, the Dutch bank paying £1.00 for it in 1995. Many of Leeson's former colleagues lost their jobs.

Barings's investors also lost out. Their misery was compounded on hearing that the bank's directors would still be getting large bonuses.

A few months later, the chancellor, Kenneth Clarke, having already said that the banking regulatory system would be 'thoroughly' reviewed, presented an eagerly awaited *Bank of England report to the Commons. The report, as expected, said that Barings's fall 'came from unauthorised and concealed trading positions,' and 'serious problems of controls and management failings within the Barings group.'*

Future business owners, executives, and entrepreneurs should pay heed to the story just told. Barings Bank, founded in 1762 in London, England, was the second oldest merchant bank when it collapsed in 1995 after incurring losses of over $1 billion caused by just one twenty-eight-year-old employee driven by making higher levels of profit and making reckless decisions on behalf of the bank in the process. If you don't think it can happen to your business, think again.

I have taken a number of personality profile assessments over my career, as have administered a very large number of them as well. To me, and I grant you this is a subjective evaluation, the best personality profile assessment I have ever come across in the past 30 plus years is the "DISC."

Described as a behavioral assessment tool based on a theory established by psychologist William Marston, the "DISC" personality profile assessment is by far the most useful to me as an executive when evaluating candidates for future employment. It is a behavioral assessment tool that focuses on four primary behavioral traits: "dominance," "influence," "steadiness," and "compliance."

a) "D"—Dominance: An employee with this personality profile is competitive, confident, likes a challenge, is blunt, sees the bigger picture, doesn't beat around the bush, and places an emphasis on accomplishing results.

b) "I"—Influence: An employee with this personality profile is optimistic, enthusiastic, likes to be in a collaborative environment, which means he or she does not want to be ignored, and places an emphasis on influencing or persuading others, openness, and relationship building.

c) "S"—Steadiness: An employee with this personality profile is calm both in manner and approach, doesn't like to be rushed, is supportive, and places an emphasis on cooperation, sincerity, and dependability.

d) "C" Compliance (Conscientiousness): An employee with this personality profile is independent, makes decisions based on objective reasoning, and places an emphasis on quality, accuracy, expertise, and competency.

The "DISC" personality profile is an extremely valuable tool for assessing an employee's potential, as well as how well they will perform in the future when confronted with differing events, circumstances, and conflicts. For example:

a) employees with personality profiles that are "D"s and "I"s have a competitive nature about them

b) employees with personality profiles that are "S"s and "C"s are more reserved

c) employees with personality profiles that are "D"s and "C"s are more task-oriented

d) employees with personality profiles that are "I"s and "S"s are more people oriented

Every organization structure that I know of, especially those found in the construction industry, has a position for at least one, if not more, of the "DISC" personality profiles, not to mention participants at a negotiating table.

a) "D" personality profiles are valuable because they are direct, blunt, competitive, and task oriented. "D"s definitely do not shy away from an argument or confrontation; however, given their inherent combative and demanding nature "D"s do not necessarily make for the most effective heads of an organization or negotiating team.

b) "I" or "S" personality profiles tend to be more conducive to filling executive and senior leadership positions of an organizational because of how they approach interpersonal relationships. "I"s or "S"s are also more suited to lead negotiation teams because of their emphasis on building consensus among opposing parties.

c) "C" personality profiles are better suited for support and technical positions due to their objective reasoning and emphasis on quality and accuracy. "C"s can be very valuable during a conflict resolution or negotiations due to their inherent desire to track of details.

So the question becomes, why is personality profiling important to being a progressive, "high performance" company?

Short answer: (a) operational alignment and (b) effective outcome created through the negotiating process.

Operational alignment is the ability of an organization to align its distinct culture comprised of "values," beliefs, attitudes and behaviors of individual personalities with its operational goals, functions, and activities. In other words, the culture of an organization emphasizes how activities and events should be carried out by its employees as they go about each day's activities and tasks in pursuit of achieving previously identified goals and performance metrics.

Time for a Mental Note

The basis for achieving operational alignment and synergy is when the organizational culture embraces the fact that no one thinks they are smarter than everyone else.

Take the Allied Forces fighting the Nazi Party in WWII for example, where there existed a central command comprised of military leaders from across the globe headed by General Dwight D. Eisenhower. One can only imagine what the world would be like today had one of General Eisenhower's commanding generals, like General George S. Patton for instance, took it upon himself, ignoring orders from central command, and invaded Russia once the Nazi Party fell throughout Europe; and if you will remember from your history studies, that's exactly what many at the time feared was going to happen.

Once the city of Berlin fell, General Patton still had command of multiple brigades of soldiers and a massive amount of artillery at his disposal. He could have very easily followed his own individual beliefs and convictions and gone rogue, defied central command, and led his troops east to conquer the Russian government. But as we all know, General Patton was a soldier's soldier, where the disciple of "command and control" could never be violated. To General Patton, the Allied Forces stood for everything right and just in the world with its ultimate goal of liberating Europe from Nazi control and dominance, not becoming an occupying force that would ultimately destroy the country of Russia.

Although General Patton, along with a number of other people at the time, had tightly held beliefs that Russia should be conquered, General Patton knew that if what the Allied Forces stood for was not preserved, and the organization structure of the military wasn't closely adhered to, chaos and anarchy would ensue with no standard of decency or decorum that other aggressors around the world would be measured against. That said, General Patton also had a very hard time dealing with people of like-mindedness saying, *"If everybody is thinking alike, then somebody isn't thinking."*

Operational alignment and synergy is an organization's ability to bring diverging thought processes together where the sum of the individual parts has a "value" far greater combined than any "value" left unto itself. It requires training and strong leadership to refocus diverging thought processes from looking inward starting with "what" a company does as opposed to looking outward from "why" a company does what it does, and more importantly, believes what it believes.

Time for a Mental Note

Operational alignment and the power of synergy can be visually seen by utilizing the human hand with its four fingers and thumb. Individually, the fingers and thumb are comparatively weak, functioning in a limited capacity and providing limited support in a self-defense situation. But once the hand becomes clinched, bringing fingers and thumb together in a unified, tightly held fist, you now have a weapon to be used in self-defense or a tool that can be used for a multitude of purposes. The same inherent strength can occur when the multiple personalities of an organization are brought together and aligned with and for a common purpose.

CHAPTER

15

Cash Flowing a Business's Future

Needless to say, I've saved the most important chapter for last. How business owners, executives, and entrepreneurs effectively manage cash flow is by far the most critical operational aspect of any business purpose. When it comes to money, everyone needs to pay attention.

Over the next decade or so technology is expected to change the financial and commercial exchange world like never before. Not only is there a revolution coming, but many think it's already started.

Forty years ago, and without the aid technology, Bank of America and a gentleman by the name of Dee Hock revolutionized the financial and commercial exchange world by introducing to consumers the first major credit card for purchasing products and services. It was called, VISA.

Since its inception in 1976, along with notable competitors like MasterCard, American Express, and Discovery, VISA and the credit card industry over the years has provided both consumers and merchants with a convenient way to transact business throughout the entire world. So much so, that once its convenience was combined with technology in the 1990s, the credit card industry has become one of the major drivers of GDP growth in the US as well as other countries.

But here's what's literally going to astound you to read. Within the coming years, there will be absolutely no need for consumers to use any form of currency or credit card whatsoever when purchasing a product or service. By the year 2030, if not within a short time thereafter, most if not all, commercial transactions will be performed through the exchange of digital currency. Digital currency that is no longer dependent upon a central bank, and, can be exchanged and/or transacted between two or more parties directly without an intermediary, verified by network nodes, and recorded in a public ledger.

As the technology of Electronic Data Interchange (EDI) continues to replace paper-based economies over the coming years, the exchange of digital currency is the reasonable next step in making commercial exchanges convenient, direct, automatic, and in real-time without any interruptions. Not only will individuals and businesses be able to transact commerce at the speed of light, but so too will governmental agencies as the global economy becomes fully integrated by the year 2050, if not before.

In knowing all this, where does that leave business owners, executives, and entrepreneurs who are trying to become progressive, "high performance" companies today and in the near future?

The first thing business owners, executives, and entrepreneurs (not to mention individuals) need to know when it comes to managing cash flow is that the future is now if you want to be providing products and services to customers tomorrow. Why? Because as most everyone knows, costs are being incurred for manpower, material, machinery, and incidentals long before a customer takes delivery of any product of service. In order to pay for pre-delivered costs being incurred, business owners, executives, and entrepreneurs are therefore required to accurately project when monies will be available to the company for reimbursement. It is in this capacity where a large number of business owners, executives, and entrepreneurs today fail, and where many more will do so in the future when the unforgiving exchange of seamless and real-time digital commerce gets enacted and becomes commonplace.

As complicated as it may seem running any business, most business owners, executives, and entrepreneurs today make it even more so by not making the management of their operation's cash flow their highest priority. Instead, most prefer to rely on a thirty-day financial report telling them how much, or how little, profit that's been recently generated.

From a cash flow perspective, let's start with the basic three step cycle of most business purposes:

a) Get work (selling)—committed to in writing
b) Do work—as efficiently as possible
c) Collecting money—as quickly as possible

Similar to the Deming Cycle of Plan, Do, Check, and Act relating to the four logical and repetitive steps for continuous process improvement, all business owners, executives, and entrepreneurs have to do is stay focused on these three repetitive steps of revenue generation in order to keep grounded in the "why," "how," and "what" of their business purpose. Pretty straightforward wouldn't you say?

However, throughout the previous chapters of this book, you've read time and again where a number of companies simply ran out of enough available funds in order to keep their businesses operating. In other words, they became illiquid, and unable to meet their current and/or short-term obligations.

"Solvency" is a term that is often times confused with "liquidity." As in the previous stories where businesses had failed in the past, many have described these companies as having been "insolvent." Terms that continue to be used interchangeably one another in an effort to describe the potential root cause of a business failure.

The term "solvency" is used when an individual or entity's current assets exceed their current liabilities, and in turn, has the ability to meet long-term obligations. However, its inverse, "insolvency," takes on a more expanded description once an individual or entity's financial situation becomes clearer and better understood.

"Insolvency" is the inability of an individual or entity to pay for obligations that owed within a specific timeframe, or, a specific moment in time. As a result, individuals and/or entities who find themselves in this particular situation are referred to as being "insolvent."

Interestingly enough, "insolvency" can be represented in one of two ways from a financial perspective: (a) balance sheet insolvency and (b) cash-flow insolvency. Balance sheet insolvency identifies the fact that an individual or entity doesn't have enough assets in order to pay for obligations that have been incurred. Cash flow insolvency is when an individual or entity has an adequate amount of assets to pay for the obligations incurred, however, said assets are not in the appropriate or convertible form of payment required to settle the obligations in full.

As for the term "liquidity." In order for an individual or entity to have "liquidity," an ability to meet current and/or short-term obligations in a form that is recognizable and acceptable to all parties to the transaction must be present at a designated moment in time. You will recall that all the companies I wrote about in the previous chapters still had ongoing operations with a considerable amount of backlog on their books with more revenue coming in the door. Theoretically this would mean that all of the companies were in a state of "solvency." However, in every case, not one of these companies had the appropriate level of "liquidity" to carry on.

In the financial world, "liquidity" is defined as the ease in which a security or asset can be bought or sold without affecting the asset's price (cash being the most liquid and hard assets like plant equipment and inventory being more on the illiquid side of the spectrum). Therefore, from an accounting perspective, "liquidity" measures the ease at which a company can meet its financial obligations so long as liquid assets are available in the short-term.

To progressive, "high performance" companies, having the ability to effectively manage working capital, along with operational cash flow requirements, ranks right up there in priority with customer relations and maintaining operational alignment and synergy. Although "solvency" and "sustainability" is what progressive, "high performance" companies are ultimately striving for long-term, progressive "high performance" companies also know without a shadow of doubt that if they are unable to achieve and maintain a required level of "liquidity," "solvency," and "sustainability" becomes irrelevant in the bigger scheme of things.

"Liquidity" is revered in such a way to progressive, "high performance" companies that close adherence to strict programs, policies, and procedures is mandatory for anyone in the organization who has the ability to influence cash flow. So much so that progressive, "high performance" companies are constantly analyzing and evaluating the amount of reserves necessary to be held on account in order to cover time sensitive trade payables and short-term obligations that might require being paid in an emergency situation in order to backstop unforeseen interruptions to their operations.

In order to meet their short-term obligations, progressive, "high performance" companies constantly evaluate their current liabilities in relation to their liquid assets through the aid of a number of ratios and financial trends. Ratios like:

- Liquidity Ratios

a) Quick Ratio = Current Assets – Inventory/Current Liability

Similar to a Current Ratio, except for the fact that a Quick Ratio looks at a company's "Quick" assets, which are considered to be highly liquid such as cash, accounts receivable, and marketable securities, as opposed to it Current Assets, which includes items like inventories that are normally a company's least liquid current asset.

b) Current Ratio = Current Assets/Current Liabilities
c) Operating Cash Flow Ratio (OCF Ratio) = Cash Flow from Operations/Current Liabilities

The Operating Cash Flow Ratio measures how well current liabilities are being covered by the cash flow generated from the business's operations. By using a business's cash flow as opposed to its income provides for a much clearer and accurate measure since earnings can be manipulated.

- AR/AP Ratio

For any specialty contractor the monthly amount of Accounts Receivable (AR) must outpace their Accounts Payable (AP) by at least a factor of two in order to insure that not only are trade payables being met, but direct labor costs as well. As an example, most commercial electrical contractor costs are proportioned as follows: 50% trade payables (AP), 40% labor, and 10% overhead & profit. Therefore, in order for the contractor every month to meet $1.00 of AP + $1 of labor cost + $1 of anticipated overhead and profit, the AR/AP ratio must be 2 at a minimum. If the contractor's monthly AR/AP ratio happens to be below 2 for this example, the contractor will not be able to meet the financial obligations of the company without some type of supplemental funding. If the AR/AP monthly trend is consistently going in a negative direction month after month, the contractor's business is very likely to fail at some point in time.

As vital as all this is to monitoring and supporting the "liquidity" of a business's operation, there is one other financial performance metric that I highly recommend for all business owners, executives, and entrepreneurs to consider using. It's called the Cash Conversion Cycle (CCC).

CCC, a.k.a. the "Cash Cycle" is a performance metric that conveys the length of time, in days, that it takes for a business to convert its resources, i.e., means, methods, material machinery, manpower, and money into cash flow. CCC attempts to measure the amount of time each resource dollar is tied up before it is converted into cash through the billing cycle.

In other words, the CCC performance metric analyzes the amount of time required for a business to sell its product or service, the length of time needed to collect its receivables, and the length of time that is afforded by venders to pay bills without incurring penalties.

The "Cash Cycle" formula is as follows:

CCC = DIO + DSO – DPO

- CCC: Cash Conversion Cycle measures the number of days a company's cash is tied up in the production and sales process of its operations and the benefit it derives from payment terms from its creditors. The shorter the cycle, the more liquid the company's working capital position is.

- DIO: Days Inventory Outstanding is a measurement of how long it takes to convert the company's outstanding inventory, e.g., for contractors this is their WIP, in to cash. The metric is calculated by dividing the company's average inventory by its costs of sales, i.e., revenue per day (shorter amount of time is preferred).

- DSO: Days Sales Outstanding is calculated by dividing the average accounts receivable figure by the net sales per day figure. DSO provides an estimate of how long it takes the company to collect on sales that go into the company's accounts receivables (shorter amount of time is preferred).

- DPO: Days Payable Outstanding is calculated by dividing the company's average accounts payable figure by its costs of sales per day. DPO provides an estimate of how long it takes the company to pay its suppliers.(longer amount of time is preferred)

So why is the "cash cycle" so important to a businesses' "liquidity"?

First, the "Cash Cycle" is an indicator of how well, i.e., efficient, the organization is managing its working capital assets; and secondly, the "cash cycle" is a more accurate prognostication of the company's ability to pay for its current liabilities.

Here's an example of what I'm talking about.

According to a *Forbes* calculation of a period running through 2012 relating to Amazon's "Cash Cycle, *"Amazon manages to hold inventory for 28.9 days plus 10.6 days to collect receivables or 40 days in total but then pays accounts payable in 54 days thus achieving a negative cash conversion cycle for Amazon.com of -14 days. You don't see this that often but definitely a win for Amazon shareholders. Maybe not for the suppliers waiting for their checks."*

As a comparison to Amazon and the online retail industry, most number of other industries like construction typically procure and hold inventory from suppliers and venders for up to 120 days, then add another 60 days to collect receivables equating to 180 days in total. But because most a number of companies like contractors view cash discounts as "found money," they are compelled to pay their venders in an accelerated manner, thus achieving a positive CCC of 150 days. Is it any wonder why companies like contractors start to become illiquid during times of revenue expansion when they're financing their costs up to almost five months at a time?

Time for a Mental Note

A shorter "cash cycle" translates into greater "liquidity," meaning an increased capacity to fund more opportunities in the future and less funds that need to be raised through a third part. A longer "cash cycle" means "liquidity" is eroding, and if allowed to continue, will progressively reduce the amount of available cash to be use to meet short-term obligations. By comparison, with a fourteen-day CCC, it easy to see why companies like Amazon have absolutely no problem with cash flow, while companies like contractors with their CCC at 150 days are constantly in a cash flow crisis.

If business owners, executives, and entrepreneurs truly want to avoid the same disastrous outcome as many of their competitors have faced in the past, I cannot stress these following points enough.

a) Business owners, executives, and entrepreneurs have got to start steering their operational culture away from relying on historically unreliable levels of profit in order to determine their company's "liquidity," "solvency," and "sustainability."

b) Business owners, executives, and entrepreneurs have got to start creating a culture based on meeting short-term cash flow needs, i.e., "liquidity," emphasizing to managerial and supervisory staffs that it is in everyone's best interest to insure that positive cash flow is maintained at all times.

c) Business owners, executives, and entrepreneurs have got to reinvent their incentive programs for operational managers and supervisors that emphasizes the need to achieve and maintain a required level of operational alignment, synergy, and liquidity, and handsomely rewarding those managers and supervisors who consistently meet or exceed cash flow requirements and standards above all else.

Background: Tampa, FL

I was the senior contract manager overseeing the electrical work of a large transit project under construction at Tampa International Airport. The project was fast track, and a project I knew I was going to have to stay on top of it, cash flow-wise, given the projected one hundred–plus people working on the project.

The prime contractor on the project mandated at the very beginning of the project that a schedule of values (SOV) be used as backup to the monthly progress billings. In other words, the construction schedule used to build the project was also to be cost loaded for ease of review each month; which is always a great idea until the project starts falling behind and the construction schedule starts getting manipulated every month by the prime contractor in order to mask any slippage in the critical path.

Luckily for me as the senior contract manager, I was provided with high-caliber people to help deliver the project. The superintendent in particular, I would put up against most superintendents I've worked with in the past when it came to means, methods, and the delivery of large, complex projects. The same can be said about the senior superintendent assigned to the project as well, who also had responsibilities overseeing a similar-sized project about one hundred miles away at the same time.

Because of the fast track nature of the project, which also had very steep liquidated damage penalties if the work wasn't finished on time, everyone's primary focus was on doing whatever it took to keep information, material, and equipment procured and delivered in time for the people installing the work. And due to this laser focus, anything not related to "building the project" was looked upon as a secondary task that would be addressed when time allowed. Secondary tasks that included critical administrative items like updating the cost loaded schedule and progress billings once a month.

As the amount of manpower increased and the need to keep the information, material, and equipment flowing as efficiently as possible, less and less time was afforded to the administrative side of things by the senior field supervisors. Each month, less and less time would be allocated by the superintendent to focus on updating the schedule and monthly progress billings, where at one point the superintendent pressed for time said, "If we don't get it [billable items] this month, we'll get it next month," referring to certain percentages of completion for activity items on the cost loaded schedule that needed final review and approval by the architect.

In other words, so long as the superintendent's paycheck got funded every week, a heightened concerned with making sure adequate amounts money came in as receivables each month to the costs being incurred at a rapid rate was not going to be a high priority of his. Needless to say, the two of us came to an understanding about the importance of cash flow.

What is critically important to note about the previous story is the fact that like most companies operating today managerial and supervisory staffs are not being properly trained on the importance of taking the time to insure certain administrative functions and/ or activities are being reported with the highest degree of accuracy; especially those relating to the cash flow needs of the company. Automation and real-time data purging will eventually take care of these inaccuracies, but until such time, reliability must fall to those in charge and responsible.

I cannot say it or stress this point enough to business owners, executives, and entrepreneurs, "liquidity" is the ability for a business to pay its obligations as they come due. In order for that to happen, it is imperative for businesses to have access to cash when it's needed and/or required. If businesses do not have the ability to pay for things they've acquired on credit, they will not be able to stay in business for very long before creditors, including employees, shut them down. It's just that simple.

ABOUT THE AUTHOR

Rodney Schultz has spent his entire career in the construction industry. For thirty plus years, Mr. Schultz has held numerous executive level positions for both construction management and specialty construction companies, responsible for project budgets as high as $100 million and payrolls in excess of 350 employees. As a contributing writer, Mr. Schultz has published a number of trade publication articles. He has also held an ownership position in a dot.com company, as well as a management consultant for a merchant banking firm from Wall Street. With an extensive background in nuclear engineering from Arizona State University, Mr. Schultz holds a Bachelor of Business Administration from the University of Missouri-Kansas City. After spending time in Japan learning the principles behind the Toyota Production System, Mr. Schultz has trained over 1,000 craftsmen, supervisors, management and staff in the techniques of World Class Quality. Mr. Schultz can always be reached at: rodneywschultz@gmail.com.

CPSIA information can be obtained
at www.ICGtesting.com
Printed in the USA
LVHW091530120320
649838LV00001BA/31